FRONT-END DESIGN FOR SYSTEMS

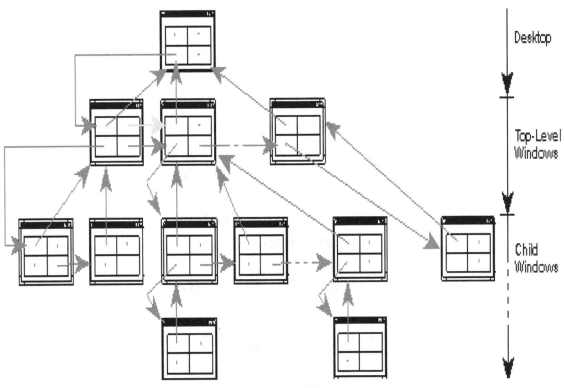

Figure 3.1.3.3 Window Hierarchy

ANDREAS SOFRONIOU

ANDREAS SOFRONIOU

ISBN: 0 9527 253 4 7

Contents:

ANDREAS SOFRONIOU

1.0 INTRODUCTION

1.1 SCOPE OF THE BOOK

This book is published with the specific purpose of setting standards and guidelines for Graphical User Interface (GUI) design and development. The book was originally a document written by PsySys Limited and it is intended to provide a guide to designing and developing the presentation layer, or 'front-end' for systems applications. A further reason for writing this book is to ensure that high standards are adhered during systems developments.

As an overall guideline, it is intended that various Microsoft Windows versions (95, 98, 2000 and XP Professional) look and feel is achieved. To this end, *The Windows Interface Guidelines for Software Design* (Microsoft Press) should be used as the definitive source of reference unless specifically overridden by sections contained in this book.

In order to define the look and feel of screens used in sub-systems, or similar groups of functionality within the applications, there is a need to define more specific standards. These standards direct the developer on the controls/widgets, screen geography, and screen navigation, to be used in certain situations. Standards for these are located in Appendices.

There will be references to Microsoft's Visual Basic 4 and other products as it is assumed that these will be the major GUI development and toolset environments.

1.2 THE HUMAN COMPUTER INTERFACE

The Human Computer Interface is the means through which users communicate with the computer system. Many types of dialogue style have been used in HCIs. A dialogue style is the combination of display elements, common types and user procedures. Dialogue styles can be divided into Graphical User Interface (GUI), in which a user points to and interacts with visible elements of the interface by using a pointing device and Character-Based User Interface (CUI). The CUI can be divided into Command Line Interface (CLI) in which a user remembers commands and types them and Menu Driven Interface, in which a user is provided with a hierarchically organised set of choices.

Today, the vast majority of users have experience with CUI on mainframes and PCs and the transfer to GUIs should be a well thought-out decision and not an act of faith. Factors like usability, productivity, standards, cost and environment could be of help in making such a switch.

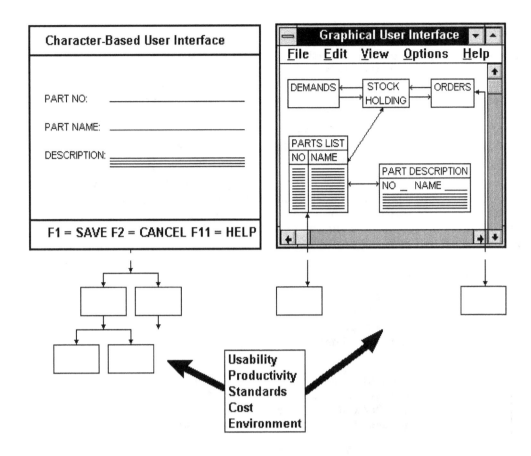

FIGURE 1.2 - SELECTION OF THE HUMAN COMPUTER INTERFACE

1.3 OBJECT ORIENTATION

GUIs are becoming more object-oriented. Object orientation, in general, is getting more popular and could be accepted widely in the near future. In Object orientation a user's focus is on objects and the concept of applications is hidden. Object-oriented user interfaces allow the development of a working environment in which each element, called an object, can interact with every other element.

Object orientation reflects the way a person works in the real world. In the GUI environment, an object is any visual component of a user interface that a user can work with as a unit, independent of other items, to perform a task. A spreadsheet, one cell in a spreadsheet, a bar chart, one bar in a bar chart, a report, a paragraph in a report, a database, one record in a database, and a printer are all objects. Each object can be represented by one or more graphic images, called icons, with which a user can interact.

1.4 USER INTERFACE BACKGROUND

In the past, many system users were technical personnel. The systems were computer-centred and the programmers' needs and expectations, rather than the users', drove the interaction between user and computer. Today, many users are less technical and see the computer as a tool to help them accomplish their tasks rather than as a part of a technical system. Therefore, it is important to ensure that the human-computer interface is highly visible. Graphical User Interface (GUI) is a major step towards improving the design of human-computer interface. Its visibility and object orientation makes it user-friendly, in comparison to previous user interfaces.

IBM published the first Common User Access (CUA) guide to interface design in 1987 and laid down the foundation for the development of the most popular GUI style in use today. Microsoft Windows (MS Windows) became popular as a bridge for MS-DOS users wishing to enter the GUI world. Motif, the Open Software Foundation's GUI is built on top of X-Windows and is based on DEC-windows. OSF/Motif and MS Windows, which are highly compatible from the user's point of view, will continue as the best-supported and most commercially prevalent GUI style for the foreseeable future.

The scope of this book is to create a GUI Style Guide in order to give a consistent look and feel across all client applications. This GUI Style Guide is intended for the application designer, not the application programmer. Guidelines for designing such applications are divided into guidelines for designing GUI and guidelines for the usage of GUI elements.

The study will identify and present general guidelines and elements that arise from the need to develop Microsoft-Windows-type look and feel for the GUIs. This GUI Style Guide concentrates on the "look and feel" aspects of the Human Computer Interface (HCI) and recommends a consistent set of Windows GUI design elements to form the GUI standards definition.

This book is drawn from a number of sources throughout the PsySys systems development cycle. It also contains elements derived from discussions with clients.

The first part of the book covers guidelines for designing a GUI. It discusses basic principles for such design. In order to illustrate the connections between the principles and GUI elements, visual examples are provided.

1.5 GUI SYSTEMS DIFFERENCES

Ideally, developers would like to write portable applications that would run on any GUI environment, especially both MS Windows and Motif, or to easily port applications from one to another. Unfortunately, programming tools and services provided by different GUI tools' vendors are different, or provide similar functionality under different names. The most obvious difference between MS Windows and Motif, as well as among all GUIs is the Application Program Interface (API).

The API is the set of functions (usually library of routines) that perform tasks such as creating windows and displaying graphics. Each system has a unique set of functions with different names, numbers of parameters and calling sequences. Many development tools comply with the international API standards, which include usage of compliant VBXs and OLE 2 technology.

Another difference is in the set of user inputs supported. Among the common user inputs are:

• Mouse movement, click down on a mouse button or release the mouse button,

• Keyboard event, generated when the user has pressed or released the key,

- Menus, generated when the user selects a command from a menu,

- Resize, which means that the user has changed the size of the window,

- Scroll event, generated when the user moves a scrollbar, indicating that the application must move the contents of the window,

- Changing the current, or active window.

Differences related to the popular displays (user output) are the following:

- Origin of the drawing space could be in the upper left corner or lower left corner,

- Resolution may be 72 Dots Per Inch (DPI), 100 DPI or a single character cell,

- Drawing algorithms differ in centring the endpoint,

- Displays differ widely in the number of colours that can be represented and in the number of bits used to specify the colour,

- GUIs treat text more like graphics, offering a rich set of display options; however, the major vendors tend to use similar features under different names, and slight modifications.

This book covers the prevalent versions of Windows available at the moment. It is assumed that the environment will be the standard desktop PC, monitor resolution of 800 x 600 (at least minimum screen size of 12 inches), mouse pointing device, QWERTY keyboard, and using the Windows 95, 98, 2000, XP Professional, Windows NT 4.0, or higher.

1.6 WINDOWING SYSTEM ARCHITECTURE

Windowing systems share many common components. However, they are different in their approach of dealing with the operating systems and hardware. There are three types of windowing system architectures:

- Kernel based windowing systems are built into the operating system. They are very efficient, but device dependent. Examples are Macintosh, NextStep and OS/2 Presentation Manager.

- Client/Server windowing system architecture is divided into two - the client GUI, and the processing server. The extent of processing may be split between the client and server as specified during the design of the system. The client program may run on the same machine or any other on the network. It is device independent, but requires additional communications overheads.

- Some windowing systems run on a single machine, like kernel based, but run on top of an operating system. Traditional MS Windows is a typical representative of this category.

1.7 BUSINESS BENEFITS

Customers may use different applications and a variety of third party applications. Therefore, the advantage of having a common look and feel across systems is obvious. By adopting a similar interface to different vendor products, applications will be easier to learn and use. Consistency minimises the need for training when new applications are introduced. The user can transfer knowledge from one product to another, as well as predict how something new will work, thanks to consistent interface design.

An object-oriented user interface provides an environment in which a user's interaction with objects is the same across tasks. As a result, end users should experience higher productivity and satisfaction, while producing fewer errors and reducing design and development costs.

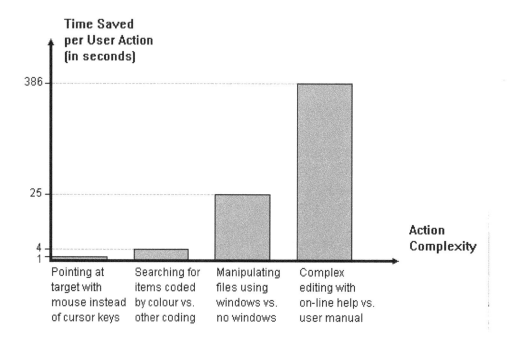

FIGURE 1.7 - HOW THE USER INTERFACE AFFECTS PRODUCTIVITY

Note:

Although colour-coding various items in an application benefits the user, this is true only to an extent, as use of increasing numbers of colours has the opposite effect. Too many colours can deter users and may therefore reduce their productivity.

2.0 GUIDELINES FOR DESIGNING GUI

2.1 PRINCIPLES

Applications continually evolve and it is impossible to provide specific recommendations that cover every possible interface. Therefore, applications should follow general or basic principles. GUIs should be designed to meet the following overall objectives:

- Increase a user's productivity,

- Increase a user's satisfaction with a product,

- Reduce a user's error rate.

In order to ensure that overall objectives are met it is essential that:

- Users can develop a conceptual model of the interface,

- Users can and should be in control of the dialogue.

A user's conceptual model is a mental model. A programmer's model and a designer's model of the HCI are explicit, consciously designed models. A diagram, or a textual description can typically represent explicit models. However, a person develops a conceptual model through experience and then develops expectations based on the relationships in the model. When confronted with a new situation, a person tries to interpret it by comparing it to an existing model. To understand a user's conceptual model, a designer must understand something about relevant user experiences (such as knowledge background and job training, as well as previous interaction with machines) and the current working environment (such as the type of hardware and system software in use). Also, a designer must understand what kinds of information a user needs and what functions a computer system should offer to help a user perform a task.

The following general design principles should be followed to optimise the design of the GUI for the users and the tasks they will perform.

- Using metaphors,

- Clarity,

- Making the interface consistent,

- Making the interface transparent,

- Internationalisation of the interface.

2.2 MAKING THE INTERFACE FLEXIBLE

Providing multiple ways to access application functions and accomplish their task increases a user's sense of control. Flexibility enables the user to select the best method of accessing a function based on the criteria the user chooses: experience level, personal preference, unique situation or something else. Typically the user can use the pull-down type of menu with cascading submenus and access keys (e.g. Ctrl+X). Toolbars are also used in conjunction with the menus - to enhance the usability and user friendliness - where a user clicks on an icon to invoke a command. A menu structure of this nature should be used.

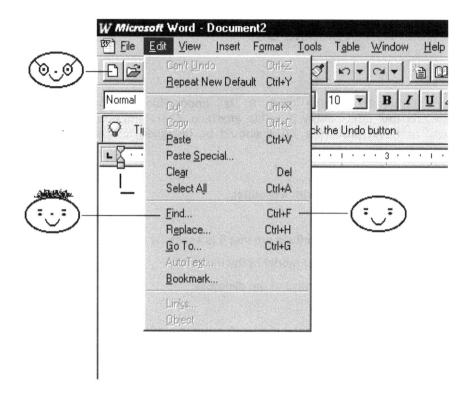

FIGURE 2.2 - ALTERNATIVE MENU OPTION, KEYBOARD SHORTCUT AND TOOLBAR COMMANDS MAKE THE INTERFACE
FLEXIBLE

2.3 GROUP ACTIONS LOGICALLY

Group objects and actions that are used together to complete user tasks within the same windows. Ensure that the sequences through the dialogue are compatible with the most likely actions to be performed by users.

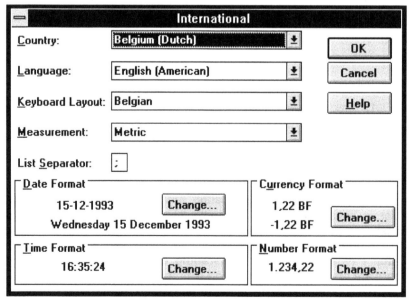

FIGURE 2.3 - GROUPING GUI ELEMENTS LOGICALLY MAKES INTERFACE EASY TO USE AND SET

2.4 TRANSPARENCY

Do not make users focus on the mechanics of an application. Users should not have to know how an application works to get a task done, as they should not have to know how a car engine works to get from one place to another. A User interface should be so simple that users are not aware of the tools and mechanisms that make the application work.

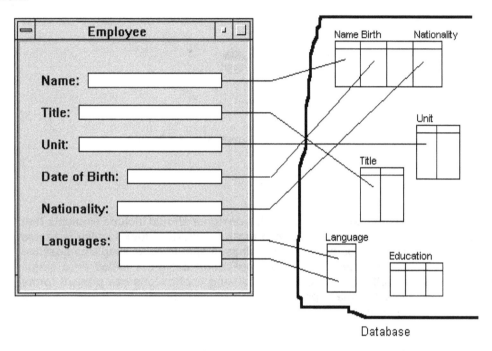

FIGURE 2.4 - DATABASE ORGANISATION IS TRANSPARENT TO THE USER

2.5 CLARITY

An application interface should be visually and linguistically clear. Spatial grouping, contrast and three-dimensional representation increase visual clarity. Linguistic clarity is increased by use of meaningful names for objects, use of meaningful actions performed on menus and use of simple text in help.

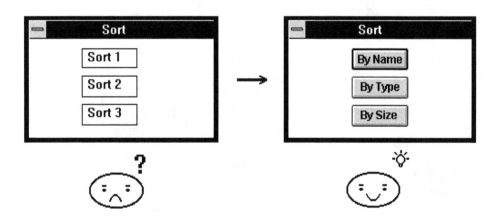

FIGURE 2.5 - VISUAL AND LINGUISTIC CLARITY

2.6 PROVIDING IMMEDIATE FEEDBACK

Always provide immediate and accurate feedback for user interactions (visual, audible or both). It is especially important for applications to give feedback for time-consuming activities.

FIGURE 2.6 - USING DIFFERENT POINTERS PROVIDES IMMEDIATE FEEDBACK

2.7 METAPHORS

To draw on a user's existing conceptual model, a designer should include elements that are familiar to a user. One way a designer can make an interface look familiar is to use metaphors. A metaphor (or analogy) relates to things. It should be as simple as possible so that the user can assimilate it. Often, an application design is based on a single metaphor. For example, billing, insurance and banking applications can present forms that are visually equivalent to the paper forms with which users are familiar. Metaphors are easily implemented in GUIs.

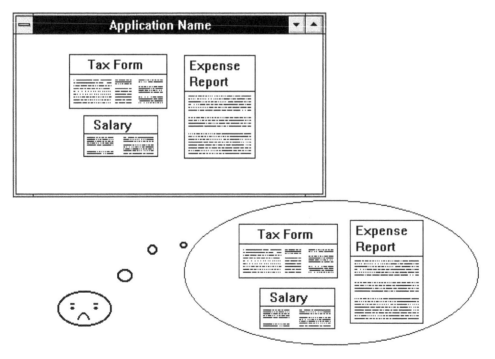

FIGURE 2.7 - METAPHORS PROVIDE A DIRECT LINK BETWEEN THE HCI AND WHAT A USER ALREADY UNDERSTANDS

2.8 MAKING THE INTERFACE VISUAL

GUIs support a wide variety of visual elements that should be used to help the user. Font types and the highlighting assist in making messages clear. Dim options that are sometimes not available, instead of removing them; this gives the user a sense of stability and consistency. Use the what-you-see-is-what-you-get (WYSIWYG) approach. To avoid overloading a user's memory, provide default settings and save previously selected settings. The window in which the settings are saved can also remind a user about which settings are in effect.

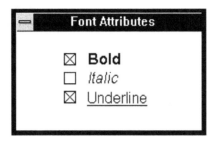

FIGURE 2.8 - USING CHECK BOXES MAKE INTERFACE VISUAL

2.9 CONSISTENCY

Consistency helps a user to transfer knowledge from one product to another and helps a user predict how something new will work. To create a consistent user interface, a designer should develop paradigms that provide identical implementation of common functions throughout a product. Be consistent within an application. Never surprise the user with a new meaning for a familiar symbol. Be consistent among applications. It allows users to learn a new application more easily. Establishing the following supports consistency in an application:

- Common presentation,

- Common interaction,

- Common process sequence,

- Common actions.

Common presentation is what users see. For example, a window title bar is consistent in both appearance and in location. Radio buttons are consistent in appearance but not in location. When you consistently support the interaction techniques associated with each component, users become familiar with these techniques. When your application consistently supports a common process sequence, users become familiar with that way to interact with the application. Common actions are, for example, when users select the OK action, they are telling the computer they have finished working with a particular window.

Occasionally, the goals of cross-platform consistency and within-platform consistency may conflict. In such cases, give the priority to within-platform consistency, because most users only work within one platform.

2.10 SUPPORT USER LEARNING

Learning can be supported explicitly through the use of appropriate prompts and help facilities. On-line help, warning and error messages are particularly important. These must be part of application development.

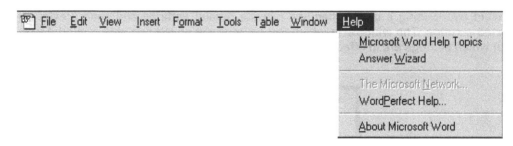

Figure 2.10 - Different Levels of Help Supports User Learning

2.11 INTERNATIONALISATION

Systems should be designed to accommodate different languages and cultures. Also, international adaptability must be catered for in the applications.

Buttons and fields must be designed to accommodate the label in the longest translation (text translated from English is likely to expand 30% to 50%). A key during design is to use the language with the longest words, so that words in other languages can only be smaller. Left justify all text fields, and headings must be justified as the text is. Create separate modules for boilerplate text (label). Do not embed text within graphics - this makes translation difficult. Some cultures do not have devices with buttons; they may not recognise buttons as controls, so allow keyboard access. Colours and symbols may have entirely different meanings in other cultures; if possible use an already existing international icon.

Each country has a different way of sorting, and may have several ways of sorting within the country; most of these options will be as defined by the set-up process of the application. Punctuation rules vary between cultures. Typically, dates and currency representation varies between countries, so greater care must be taken in designing the application to cater for this. Although the general format of the date and time representation can be set in the Windows' Control Panel, and subsequently be used in the application for basic interpretation for the country-specific formats, it will be advisable to use a translation table for a greater depth of internationalisation.

A translation table will allow text to be displayed on the screens in the local language and formats, while allowing developers to develop common code. Microsoft uses the concept of resource files. Some organisations provide the additional feature of geometry management where multi-lingual screens adapt to the appropriate language in terms of sizing and field orientation.

Errors should also be treated in the same way, where local language error messages are displayed. Some development tools allow messages to be tailored at lower levels, e.g. have database translation tables.

Allow users to select units of measure; inches and pounds are not used in the metric system.

In some languages (Hebrew or Arabic) the scanning direction is from right to left. (But, for this book the emphasis will be European adaptability). People currently living in the countries where the interface will be used should evaluate languages and custom changes. Choosing the language and territory sets these up, i.e. Canadian French will be different from French in France.

A significant development in Europe that is most likely to impact future development is the evolution of a common European currency, currently called the 'Euro'. It is possible that for a period of time there could be parallel currencies in use in each country with a potential big-bang switch to the common currency at a later date. This raises a dilemma - to store just the local currency (with the need for subsequent conversion), or dual amounts from the outset of a contract. The general direction for editable text and character sets should be the Euro character set.

It should be noted that in some organisations screens could resize according to the length of labels associated with them. However, it should be pointed out that tabs are not re-sizeable.

For address handling, there will be a country specific input mask that needs to be defined for each country to control address input.

The discussion on the requirements and specification of internationalisation standards is an on-going theme.

2.11.1 Monetary Fields

- Maximum monetary amount without consolidation will be 15 digits (including two digits for fractions of whole currency), for example, 'customer receivable',

- Maximum monetary amount on the first consolidation level will be 17 digits (including two digits for fractions of whole currency), i.e. 'customer receivable',

- Maximum monetary amount on the second consolidation level will be 18 digits (including two digits for fractions of whole currency), i.e. 'customer receivable'. The intended length of 19 cannot be used due to restrictions of the COBOL compiler,

- Transactions will be entered using a debit/credit format.

2.11.2 Currency

- All base screens will be shown in contract/country currency,

- All interfaces will be handled in local currency,

- All legal rounding strategies will be handled on a country currency basis.

2.11.3 Dates

- Formatting will be based on the country of the user's preference. A default screen format will be set at DD/MM/CCYY,

- Key entry of dates by user will only be numeric. If the century is not entered, the system will insert the century of the system date (CC will default to system date),

- Reporting dates will be based on country formatting requirement with CCYY.

2.12 INFORMATION FORMATTING

The screen or GUI will constitute many controls (widgets) which express information in particular ways, for which more detail can be found in Section 3.3.3.2, Controls. It is important (and should be included in development) for any widget that allows input to be intelligent in some ways.

For example:

• Provide validation to prevent erroneous data from being input, and this extends to checking for case sensitive text and checking against valid character sets or strings. For monetary data it should not be necessary for the user to input the currency symbol, decimal, or other separators, as it will be easier to update and validate the raw data. For displaying monetary data, the currency symbol, decimal, and other separators will be necessary.

• Provide rounding facilities for numeric data to prevent excessive or incorrect data updating the database tables. The rounding criteria and algorithms depend on the specifications of the project, and could even be country-specific.

• Navigation processing occurs when the widget gains or losses focus. The processing depends on the specifications of the project, but it should be noted that only basic processing must be carried out at the client side, with bulk processing occurring at the server or second business tier to improve performance.

2.13 PROVIDE SHORTCUTS

A designer can provide a way for a user to go beyond the basic level of knowledge required for frequently used features to allow experienced or 'power' users to have the best of both worlds. Remember, however, that shortcuts should never be the only way to access a feature.

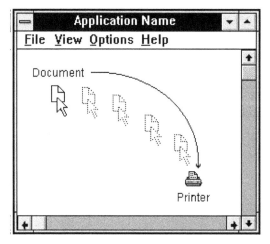

FIGURE 2.13 - EXAMPLE OF DIRECT MANIPULATION BY MOVING THE DOCUMENT TO THE PRINTER

2.14 REDUCE THE NEED FOR USERS TO REMEMBER INFORMATION

As people are better at recognition than at recall, a product should present alternatives and let a user choose from among them. Whenever possible provide users with a list of items from which they can choose instead of making them recall valid choices. Provide all the information that a user needs at each point, either within a single window, or by providing default displays of all the windows in non-overlapping form. Provide rapid access to objects that a user may need to complete a form or to select data.

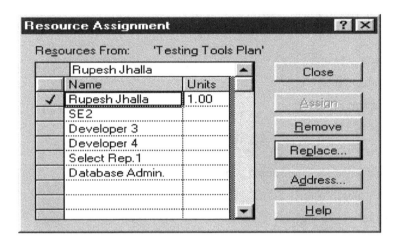

FIGURE 2.14 - POP-UP MENU REDUCES THE NEED FOR USERS TO REMEMBER

2.15 MAKING THE INTERFACE FORGIVING

Users like to learn by trial and error. The interface should accommodate user's exploration and mistakes without pain or penalty. Their actions should be easily reversed. They should be able to back up or undo their previous action. Warn users about all actions that are irreversible or risky, and allow them to cancel these actions.

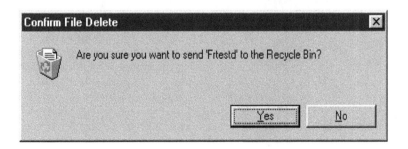

FIGURE 2.15 - WARNING DIALOG BOX MAKES INTERFACE FORGIVING

2.16 USER CONTROL

The key element in GUI programming is the assumption that the user wants to be and should always be in control. Users are in control when they are able to switch from one activity to another and stop an activity they no longer want to continue. Therefore, the application must be structured to deal with asynchronous user inputs at any time. It should also be able to allow users to cancel or suspend any time-consuming activity without causing disastrous results.

The techniques that put users in control are:

- Making the interface flexible,

- Making the interface forgiving,

- Making the interface visual,

- Providing immediate feedback,

- Group actions logically,

- Reduce the need for users to remember information,

- Support user learning,

- Provide shortcuts.

These techniques are to be adopted on a case-by-case basis, where the detailed requirements will define the precise application.

3.0 GUIDELINES FOR USING GUI ELEMENTS

3.1 PRESENTATION

Presentation is what users see on the screen. In general, applications present to users two types of information: objects and actions. Objects are the focus of users' attention and can be composed of sub-objects. Actions modify the properties of an object (for example the layout of selected text in text processor) or manipulate the object. The container that holds all objects in the GUI is called the workspace, desktop, or canvas, depending on the development tool being used. It fills the entire screen and serves as a background for a user's work. Primary visual components of the GUI presentation are windows, icons and pointers.

It is important to understand that some Windows development tool approaches certain aspects of GUI development differently, compared to other tools, although on the whole other products do provide almost all the necessary features to deliver the desired application. The main differences are the type of widgets that are offered by other software, which have the look and feel of Visual Basic widgets, but have different names.

3.1.1 Window

A window is an interface component for presenting objects and actions to users. Windows are designed to serve the following purposes:

* To provide rapid access to more information,

* To access independent sources of information in multiple windows and combine them,

* To enable users to control several tasks at the same time,

* To remind the user about frequently used information or information likely to be of use in the future.

Basic window operations are: moving, resizing, closing, splitting windows into panes, switching between windows or panes and scrolling data in windows or panes. Only one window is active at a time.

3.1.2 Window Components

Typical Microsoft Windows based window components are:

* Title bar,
* Window border,
* Menu bar,
* Client area,
* Scroll bar,
* Status bar,
* Toolbar.

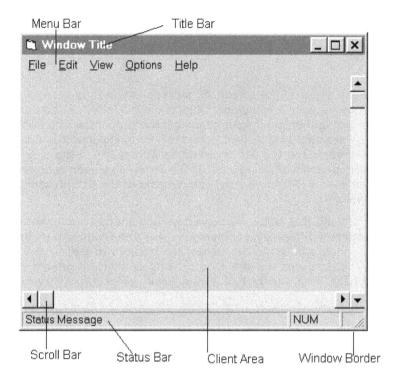

Figure 3.1.2 Windows Sample Window

3.1.2.1 Scroll Bars

Applications should provide scroll bars for all windows in which the size of the data may exceed the size of the window. Scroll bars give users a visual cue that more information is available.

3.1.2.2 Window Border

There are two types of window borders: sizeable and non-sizeable. Each type is visually distinctive. When the pointer is moved over the border, it changes into an appropriate pointer shape. The minimum size of the border should be set in the window classes where possible; use the default where Visual Basic is being used. The default of the borders should be non-sizeable, but there may be justified cases where sizing is allowed, depending on the specification of the application.

3.1.2.3 Status Bar

The status bar and message line displays information about the current state of the application. Provide a status bar for each window in which it is useful to display information about the current state of an object or view displayed in the window. The status bar will contain the following information:

- Application date - on the right-hand side of the status bar, the current Application date will be displayed.

- Status Bar Messages - the status bar will be used to display textual information to assist the user, i.e. Hint Text relating to specific fields within the window, and Toolbar Button / Drop down menu hints.

In both cases, information displayed will be dependant on the precise positioning of the mouse pointer within the window, i.e. On the Toolbar button or over an input field (for messages relating to Menu options it can also be driven by the highlighted item, where the menu has been accessed via the keyboard rather than the mouse).

3.1.2.4 Menu Bar

The menu bar (also called the action bar) on the main application menu window contains the actions of an application. It is a horizontal list of routing choices, positioned directly below the title bar. When a user selects a choice from a menu bar, an associated pull-down menu is displayed. The name of each choice on a menu bar indicates what kinds of choices appear in the associated pull-down menu. By naming the choices descriptively, a designer encourages a user to learn by exploring.

3.1.2.5 Title Bar

The window title bar consists of three parts: the system menu icon, the window title and the window-sizing icons. Users can select the system menu icon to display a pull-down menu containing the actions. Windows-sizing icons provide a fast way to minimise, maximise or restore the window size.

The title should be displayed together with any parameters that are passed into the window e.g. Customer code, Agreement number, etc. This will serve to denote the current context of the form. The title should contain, first the sub-system/functional name, followed by the parameters. Care should be taken to ensure that suitable business related titles are used.

3.1.2.6 Client Area

The client area is the part of the window inside the border, below the menu bar. User performs most application-level tasks in the client area.

3.1.2.7 Toolbars

Optional toolbars should be made available for all primary windows. The toolbar should be enabled or disabled by the use of an option on the *View* drop-down menu. Items on the toolbar should duplicate the function of some, or all of items available in the drop-down menus for a given window. Note that it is possible to have a menu item that has no toolbar equivalent, but not vice versa.

Standard Microsoft icons should be used where possible on the toolbar. Additional bit map images will need to be developed where no Microsoft equivalent is available.

Toolbar

FIGURE 3.1.2.7 TOOLBAR IN A MICROSOFT APPLICATION

3.1.3 Design Considerations in Windows

It is extremely important to maintain a consistent use of colour, fonts and user interface elements through all windows within the application. Make any window that does not currently have input focus an inactive window. Provide a split window when it is useful for a user to display a view of an object in different panes of a window.

3.1.3.1 Windows Size

The initial size and location of the primary window depends on the amount of space required by the application. Usually, this is less than the full size of the screen. Any operation, which is carried out on the window, apart from closing it, should not change its size, but it should be possible to minimise the window. To ensure that windows fit on the screens of different size, 800 x 600 pixels is recommended as a maximum window size.

3.1.3.2 Pointers

The pointer (or cursor) is a small graphical object that users move around the display using the mouse or keyboard. Typically, only one pointer appears on the workspace at a time, and it is associated with a user's pointing device. Changing pointer shape is an easy way to indicate a special action or state, and must be used at all times in the appropriate circumstances (idle pointing, application busy, printing, etc.). Pointer images that should be used in all GUIs are:

- Selection pointer,
- Text insertion,
- System busy.

    Suggested selection pointer over items

    Suggested selection pointer for left margin

↓   Suggested pointer for top of table column

FIGURE 3.1.3.2/1 - MS WINDOWS SUGGESTED SELECTION POINTERS

I   I-beam pointer; suggested for text

FIGURE 3.1.3.2/2 - MS WINDOWS SUGGESTED TEXT POINTER

Suggested pointer for graphics resizing

Suggested pointer for resizing row width

Suggested pointer for resizing column width

Suggested pointer for resizing window vertically

Suggested pointer for resizing window horizontally

Suggested pointer for resizing window diagonally (lower left or upper right)

Suggested pointer for resizing window diagonally (upper left or lower right)

FIGURE 3.1.3.2/3 - MS WINDOWS SUGGESTED POINTERS FOR RESIZING

Suggested pointer for unconstrained movement

Suggested pointer for vertical movement

Suggested pointer for horizontal movement

Suggested pointer for vertical or horizontal movement

FIGURE 3.1.3.2/4 - MS WINDOWS SUGGESTED MOVEMENT POINTERS

Suggested for indicating operation in progress

Suggested for activating associated help

Suggested for zoom inside window

Suggested for indication that direction keys will move or resize window

Suggested for indicating that dropping is not allowed

Suggested for splitting window horizontally

Suggested for splitting window vertically

FIGURE 3.1.3.2/5 - MS WINDOWS OTHER SUGGESTED POINTERS

3.1.3.3 Window Types

There are two basic types of windows: primary and supplemental:

- A primary window is a movable, sizeable top-level application window (in most cases the MDI/parent), which is the main focus for the users' work activity. The goal of an application is to provide the most frequently used actions in the client area of the primary window. All other windows created by the application are associated with the primary window

- Supplementary windows are secondary windows and dialogue boxes, including pop-up windows for messages and queries. A secondary window is a movable, sizeable window that is always associated with a primary window. These windows can be modal or modeless:

  - A modal window must be closed (hidden or unloaded) before you can continue working with the rest of the application. For example, a dialog box is modal if it requires you to click OK or Cancel before you can switch to another form or dialog box.

  - Modeless windows let you shift the focus between the window and another form without having to close the window. For instance, you can continue to work elsewhere in the current application while the dialog box is displayed. Use modeless dialog boxes to display frequently used commands or information.

The desktop window occupies the first level of the windows hierarchy and top-level windows occupy the second level. Child windows, which are windows created with the WS_CHILD style (in Visual Basic), occupy all other levels. The window manager in the Windows environment connects child windows to their parent window in the same way it connects top-level windows to the desktop window.

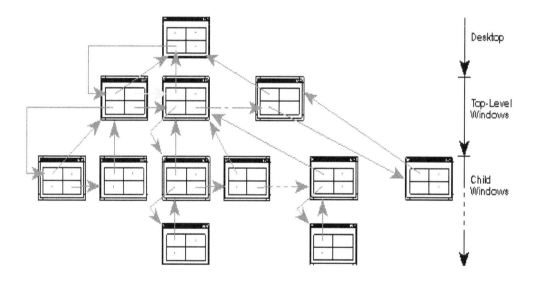

FIGURE 3.1.3.3 WINDOW HIERARCHY

3.1.3.4 Icons

Icons are small pictures that typically represent applications or windows that are temporarily minimised or processes that are time-consuming. An icon need not be a static image. It can be an animated image or even a video image. The pictures should be recognisable and easy to differentiate. The name of the icon should also be displayed. Icons can be used as buttons if an icon or graphic can easily describe the action or function related to the button.

Appropriate pointers must be displayed to show the activity on the screen, e.g. "working", loading screen, just pointing, etc.

3.1.3.5 Colour and frames

Colour should be used only for emphasis, not for additional information. Avoid using Colour when other identification techniques are available, such as location. In general, use white or low saturated Colours for backgrounds and blue for detail and emphasis. Use the Colours consistently across the application. Use the same Colour for similar functions. For example, light grey is used to indicate the unavailability of components.

3.1.3.6 Fonts

Default fonts and styles should be chosen to be compatible with Windows 95/Windows NT 4.0. It is important to choose fonts that have similar spacing and height characteristics across platforms. Do not use bold fonts, except in the title bar of a window. Minimise the number of different fonts in the window, typically only one type of font, throughout the application. But where absolutely necessary, do not use more than three fonts per window.

Use Sans Serif on graphical displays, and MS Sans Serif 8 point should be used as a general principle. Use fixed-width fonts, such as Courier, on character based displays (probably none in the P1500 Retail/Leasing applications).

Capitalisation should also follow the latest Microsoft standard which defines a combination of book title and sentence capitalisation Book title capitalisation means that the first letter of each word is capitalised unless it is an article or preposition not occurring at the beginning or end of the phrase, or unless the word's conventional usage is not capitalised.

For example:

- Insert Object,
- Paste Link,
- Save As,
- Go To,
- Always on Top,
- By Name.

Use book title capitalisation for the following circumstances:

- Text in menus,
- Command buttons,
- Tabs,
- Default names provided for file names,
- Title bar text (Bold),
- Icon labels.

Sentence capitalisation requires that only the first letter of the phrase is capitalised as well as any other word that is normally capitalised. For example:

- Extended (XMS) memory,

- Working directory,

- Print to,

- Find whole words only.

Use sentence capitalisation for field labels such as those used for the following controls:

- Option buttons,

- Check boxes,

- Text boxes,

- Group boxes,

- Radio buttons.

Use left justification for captions, characters, dates, and headers; right justification for numbers, and data oriented justification for column headers. Alignment of column headers should be according to the data they pertain to. Text for Radio Buttons and Check Boxes should be positioned to the right of the control. Omit periods when possible (USA instead of U.S.A.) and be consistent with abbreviations. Avoid hyphenation - if a word does not fit on one line, move it to the next line.

3.1.3.7 Windows Layout

Generally, windows, which are as simple as possible, make finding information and entering values more efficient. Use only the number of elements that are necessary to support the windows' functional capability. If an activity has too many elements to place in a single window, divide the elements into multiple forms. Consider placing special, less used elements, in pop-up menus. To access the additional information, use the menu bar or push buttons.

3.1.3.8 Group Boxes

Group boxes should be used for logically grouping data. An inset rectangle should be used to denote a region of related data items. A heading should be included inside the upper left-hand corner of the rectangle if the purpose of the grouping is not entirely obvious or further description will aid understanding.

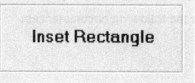

FIGURE 3.1.3.8 GROUP BOX FOR DATA/WIDGETS

3.1.4 Window Management

The best standards of screen management should be used within the capabilities of the toolset. Since the accepted P1500 Presentation Layer policy is to follow Microsoft Windows 95 "look-and feel" standards, MDI type behaviour should be used as much as is possible within the toolset. The emphasis is not, therefore, on MDI screens or Windows as used by Microsoft applications, but an attempt to be as close as possible.

Below is an outline of the basic nature of screen management required for the P1500 applications:

• The application's main menu allows functions to be invoked, but there will not be a strict parent-child relationship. This is clarified below.

• After the application's main menu, each function called from the main menu will exercise a hierarchical (and modal) screen structure. The called screens (sub-functions) will be closed if the calling screen is closed. So the emphasis is on modal-type window management. Strict modal implementation is not advised, as it will prevent simultaneous use of windows that belong to other functions and applications.

• More than one functional screen can be opened from the main menu, and the screens can be situated anywhere on the desktop, i.e. not necessarily within a parent window container of the main application.

• When the main application menu is closed, all function screens of the application should be closed, i.e. do not leave any functional screen open or existing when the main menu is closed. PanCredit support the view that the main application menu can be closed without affecting the function screens, i.e. the function screens may remain open. The former statement should be used as the current standard.

• The main menu screen can be minimised without affecting any the other function screens, i.e. the function screens may remain open on the desktop. When the main menu screen is minimised, it will appear as a button on the Windows 95 taskbar - this should be default Windows 95 behaviour.

• The main menu toolbar should be used as the basis for toolbars that will be shown for all the functions and hierarchies under them. The toolbar buttons will be greyed out as necessary for the individual screens.

3.1.4.1 Use of Command Buttons

Command buttons are used on windows in order to carry out actions that will affect the database (in the case of update/delete transactions). The following guidelines should be used for the 'OK', 'Cancel', 'Save', 'Apply' and 'Exit' buttons:

• OK should be identified as the default, will save changes, and close the screen. This button will be retained on all screens where an item may be selected and/or data changed. Where the screen will display data dependent upon the selection of an identifier, e.g. dealer name/number, RSC, G/L date, VIN/Ref. No., etc., the key information must be entered into the field and the search will be invoked by clicking on the OK button.

  Where there are changes to the underlying data (not to the search criteria themselves), the action of clicking on the OK button can be thought of as analogous to the use of the "save" button on the toolbar, i.e. the screen data will be validated and (subject to a confirmation message) the changes should be saved/committed.

  The exception to this is where there is a "long-lived" transaction, e.g. a volume transaction, which lasts over a number of screens, the order of which being critical.

In this case the action of clicking on the OK button will validate the screen and move on to the next screen in the series. The transaction will only be committed when all of the necessary screens have been completed.

It will be possible, on certain screens, e.g. to maintain specific payments or items of volume, to drill down to lower level screens by selecting the required item from a list box and then pressing OK, this being a general equivalent to double click in a grid/list.

- The Cancel button will be retained on all screens where an item may be selected and/or data changed. The action of clicking on the Cancel button can be thought of as analogous to the use of the "undo" button on the toolbar. This will lead to any pending changes on the screen being discarded, subject to a confirmation message. The action of the Cancel button will apply automatically to situations where the screen times-out.

The Cancel button will, in effect, close the window without saving.

- Save will cause the screen data to be validated and (subject to a confirmation message) the changes will be saved/committed. This occurs where there are changes to the underlying data (not to the search criteria themselves) pending. Unlike the OK button, Save will only save the changes and not close the screen. The save command can be invoked from the menu bar as well.

- The Apply button will be used where large changes are to be made to existing or open windows, and the data must first be double-checked before making the changes. Also, where it is possible to make many changes and it is likely that the user will not want to exit the window should have an Apply button. This arrangement is most common on Tab Cards where the buttons control a number of Tabs. The Apply button will allow changes to a particular Tab to be confirmed without leaving the window. The user may then go on to select further Tabs without having to re-enter the window. The button will be used in only few situations.

- Exit should be achieved by utilising menu option File, then within this the option Exit, or by clicking the close window icon on the top right corner of the window (x). The Exit button should be provided mainly to close windows, rather than trigger any processing as mentioned for other buttons. If changes were made, a pop-up window should ask the user if changes are to be saved.

3.2 FEEDBACK

Users should receive immediate feedback from the system. Graphical and textual feedback is particularly effective, but audible feedback is also useful. Textual feedback is usually in the form of messages in dialog or message boxes.

3.2.1 Handling Errors

Errors should be handled with a self-explanatory message that helps users to solve the problem. Limit the message to two or three lines. When errors occur, whether or not the users cause them, the error message should appear within the environment. Users should never find themselves in an alien environment when an error occurs. Do not allow an erroneous action to be completed. Issue a warning or action message. Try to initiate a dialog with the user to correct the error. In designing error messages be clear and specific. Use a positive tone and avoid words such as illegal, invalid or fatal. Instruct the user how to correct the error. For example if the user enters a number that is too large, the error message should say "Please enter a number between 1 and 10" instead of the message "Number too big".

Types of errors are system errors (for example, Disk is full), application errors (for example, Cannot find the file) or user errors (for example, invalid character in file name). Prevent errors of selection by disabling the choice in a menu or on push buttons and incapacitating the option. For entry fields only the label is disabled. The cursor cannot navigate into the disabled field.

Scenarios where there are multiple errors and the users must correct each error before any further processing can continue, provide the user with an updated list of errors each time the OK, Next, Close (or similar) buttons are pressed.

Basic errors such as checking for correct entry of characters, numerics, dates, etc., should be carried out at the widget level. Errors pertaining to inter-dependent widgets and functionality should be produced and reported to the user. Screen level errors should be produced where the business rules are used for validating the overall data within the screen, some of which will be checking dates, values, and calculations are within range or other criteria before updating.

Error messages in languages other than English must be produced where the specification is to use the local language. The text of the error message will be retrieved from a translation table.

3.2.2 Graphical Feedback

Graphical feedback is used when users request that the computer performs a certain operation, but it cannot satisfy the request immediately. Two methods are frequently used to inform users that an application is unavailable or busy: changing the mouse pointer or displaying a progress indicator.

The application should change the shape of the mouse pointer to an hourglass when an operation in progress takes more than two seconds and the user cannot continue working until the operation finishes. When the mouse pointer is an hourglass, all fields except the cancel operation should be prevented from accepting commands.

For complex requests, typically those that take longer than 5 seconds, a progress indicator or working dialog should be displayed to keep users informed of the status of their requests. This is optional as a very friendly feature. But employing different cursor types can also, indicate progress.

The best progress indicators are graphical. If graphical indicators take too long to update, a percentage-complete message can be used as a supplement. If percentage cannot be calculated in advance, only messages should be displayed.

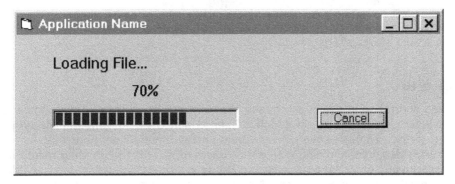

FIGURE 3.2.2 - WINDOWS GRAPHICAL PROGRESS INDICATOR

3.2.3 Audible Feedback

Audible feedback is a beep from the computer that either warns the users that they have performed an erroneous action or draws the users' attention to a certain situation or specific information. For example, if the user scrolls to the top of the data and clicks the up scroll arrow or presses the up arrow key, the system can beep instead of displaying a message. Sound should always supplement visual feedback, but should not be the only way of notifying the user. Provide audible feedback with warning and action messages. When users type a character that is not a valid mnemonic in a selection field or when users attempt to select unavailable (greyed) choices you can warn them with a beep. Always allow users the option to turn off the sound.

3.2.4 Textual Feedback

Dialog boxes and message boxes are the main forms of textual feedback.

Because text tends to grow when you localise an application, you should pay special attention when designing the following user interface (UI) components:

- Messages,
- Menus and dialog boxes,
- Icons and bitmaps.

English text strings are usually shorter than equivalent text strings in other languages. The following table shows the additional average growth for strings, based on initial length. This data is drawn from past Visual Basic localisation projects and describes an average growth rate.

English length (in characters)	Additional growth for localised strings
1 to 4	100%
5 to 10	80%
11 to 20	60%
21 to 30	40%
31 to 50	20%
Over 50	10%

When designing the interface, consider these growth ratios and allow for text to wrap to more lines, as the messages get longer.

3.2.4.1 Dialog Box

A dialog is a controlled interaction between the user and the system. A dialog box is a movable window, fixed in size, in which a user is asked for information required to complete an action. There are two types of dialog boxes: modal and modeless. A modal dialog box provides a serial dialog with which users must finish interacting before they can interact with any other window. A message box is a type of modal dialog box that is used for displaying messages to users. A modeless dialog box is a parallel dialog from which users may do something else before they complete the dialog. A modeless dialog box allows users to repeatedly perform an action without having to re-initiate the dialog. A Find dialog box is a good example of a modeless dialog box. A dialog box consists of:

- Title bar,

- Non-sizeable window border,

- Push buttons.

The dialog box related to an item in an underlying window will be positioned in the centre of the window. The size should be as small as possible to contain all information without the need for scrolling.

Every dialog box should contain at least one push button that closes the dialog. Usually a dialog box has a minimum of two push buttons (one that closes the dialog and initiates an action, and the other that closes the dialog without initiating any action). Place the push buttons horizontally in the lower part of a dialog box, or vertically at the right side of the dialog box. Push buttons that are arranged horizontally should be the same height and push buttons that are arranged vertically should be the same width. When you display several push buttons in the same dialog box, identify one of them as the default action by using a bold border. The default is usually the command button that is most often used. In cases where the most often used action is potentially destructive, cancel is often the default. You should use an ellipse (...) in push buttons when the action associated with the push button results in another dialog box. Standard push buttons in dialog boxes are:

- Action: Performs the action implied by its text (for example, Print),

- OK: Causes the application to accept any changed information in the

 dialogue box,

- Reset: Cancels any user changes that have not been submitted to the

 application,

- Cancel: Closes the dialog box without performing uncommitted user changes,

- Help: Displays, if available, contextual help for the item.

These are helpful and repetitive tasks, and there will be others as the business and technical specification is developed, which must be part of the template.

It is recommended to position first any application-specific push buttons, including OK and Reset and follow them with Cancel and Help. If changes cannot be reversed, use the Close push button instead of Cancel.

3.2.4.2 Common Dialog Boxes

Common dialog boxes in MS Windows are Open, Save As... and Print for opening, saving and printing files, and New for creating new documents.

3.2.4.2.1 Save As...

The Save As dialog box is displayed when users select the Save As... choice in the File pull-down.

The Save As dialog box is similar in appearance to the Open dialog box, except that the files list box underneath the File Name entry field is dimmed and non-selectable, although still scrollable. Also, instead of List Files of Type the label Save File as Type is used. Note that the user must enter the file name in the File Name entry field.

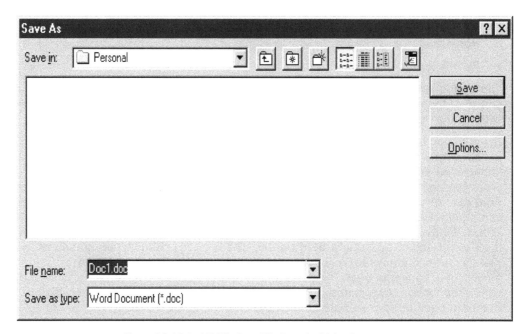

Figure 3.2.4.2.1 - MS Windows File Save As Dialog Box

3.2.4.2.2 Print

In the Print Range group box the user can choose the whole document or just a part of it. Print Quality has to be set up according to the printer device driver resolution. Print to File opens a new dialog box for the name of the file in which to print. The Collate Copies check box is turned on by default. On page-oriented printers, printing all the copies of the first page before going on to the second page is faster, so users can turn off this check box to speed up printing. The Setup... button brings up the print Setup dialog box. The Option button brings the dialog box for including application specific options.

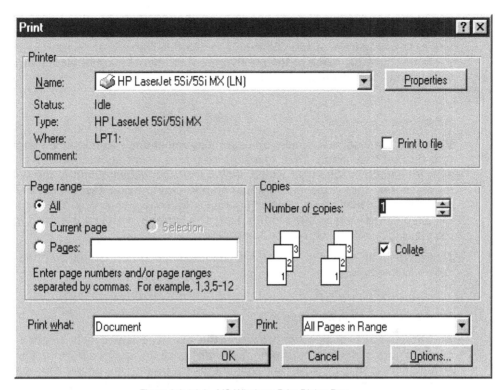

Figure 3.2.4.2.2 - MS Windows Print Dialog Box

An application should check if the printer is available and if not, display a message. The message should also be displayed if the default printer does not support the format in which the document was stored.

3.2.4.2.3 Open...

The Open dialog box is displayed when the user selects the Open... choice from the File pull-down.

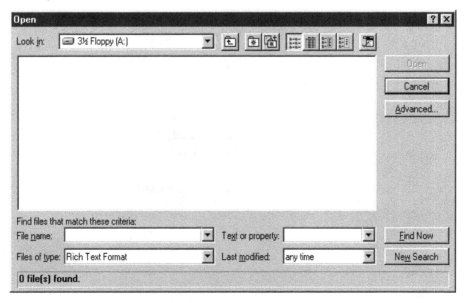

FIGURE 3.2.4.2.3 - MS WINDOWS FILE OPEN DIALOG BOX

Below the list of drives/directories is a list that contains the file names in the currently selected directory. The Files of Type allows a choice of different file types. At the bottom of the client area is the File Name entry field into which users may type the name of the file they want to open. This part also allows the user to enter search criteria to locate files.

3.2.4.2.4 Message Box

Messages are feedback, which tell users that something has happened because of a request they made. Each message box component should have: a unique icon for each message type which allows users to visually identify the type of message, text that explains the situation and may provide assistance, and the push buttons which allow users to interact with the message box. The icon is at the left and the message text to the right. The buttons are usually located below the message, with the default button outlined.

Three types of message boxes are standardised: information, warning and action message box.

3.2.4.2.5 Information Message Box

An information message box contains the message which tells users that a computer function is performing normally or has performed normally, the information icon ("i" icon) and an OK push button so users can tell the computer they are aware of the situation described in the message box. A Help push button is optional. Display an information message when a situation has occurred that the user can do nothing about or when there is additional information about the status of normal completion. Do not include a beep. Examples of appropriate messages are:

- Update (edit or calculation) requested, but no fields changed,
- Update (edit, calculation, processing; add or delete) complete,
- No information found for this request.

FIGURE 3.2.4.2.5 - WINDOWS INFORMATION MESSAGE BOX

3.2.4.2.6 Action Message Box

An action message box contains the message that tells users that an exception condition has occurred and if possible, should suggest an action to correct it (users must perform an action to correct the situation), an icon (standard stop-sign icon) and Retry and Cancel push buttons. Retry directs the application to attempt again to complete the process that caused the message, and Cancel only removes the message without any action. When an exception occurs, a product needs to tell a user at least three things: how severe the situation is, how soon the user must respond and what actions the user can take to correct the situation. Typical methods for notifying a user about an exception include audible, visual and textual cues. Examples of appropriate messages are:

* Field require input. Please enter,
* Invalid User ID. Please re-enter,
* Invalid password. Please re-enter,
* Field must be numeric (or alphanumeric). Please re-enter,
* "From" and "To" dates are required. Please enter.

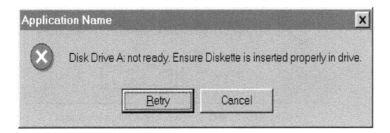

FIGURE 3.2.4.2.6 - WINDOWS ACTION MESSAGE BOX

3.2.4.2.7 Warning Message Box

A warning message box contains a message that tells users that a potentially undesirable situation could occur, the warning icon ("!" icon) and OK and Cancel or Yes and No push buttons; OK is used in conjunction with Cancel and Yes in conjunction with No. Both OK and Yes give a positive response to a question, while Cancel and No give a negative response. Include a beep. Examples of appropriate messages are:

* Record already exists,
* User not authorised to perform this function,
* Field contains invalid character (or selection). Please re-enter.

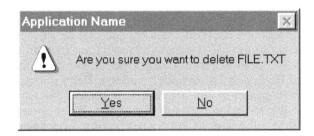

FIGURE 3.2.4.2.7/1 - WINDOWS WARNING MESSAGE BOX

As a principle, a Microsoft designer avoids the use of the question mark symbol, since the severity of the question is not clear. Error, warning or information symbols are used instead.

Some organisations make use of the following box design:

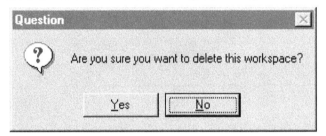

FIGURE 3.2.4.2.7/2 QUESTION DIALOG BOX FOR WINDOWS

3.3 INTERACTION

Interaction is the means through which users interact with the user interface components. GUIs use the point-and-select concept, which can be controlled by either the keyboard or mouse. Object selection should be a simple act and the user should always immediately see a visual indication that selection has occurred. Users should be able to cancel a wrong selection or change their mind without penalty. An object should remain selected even after an action has been performed on it. The object is therefore already selected for another action. Action selection should also be followed by an immediate visual indication.

3.3.1 Keyboard Interaction

The keyboard should be used as an alternative to using the mouse for navigation and execution of commands within the screens in the GUI environment. Most of the methods of using the keyboard should follow the MS Windows intuitive/default standards. A useful feature is to provide the users of the application with information on short-cut keys, which are usually shown in the menu options. The following suggestions or recommendations will be adhered to as default, and alternatives applied only in justifiable cases.

3.3.1.1 Shortcut Keys (Accelerators)

Keyboard shortcuts, or accelerators, allow users to issue menu commands from the keyboard. In this way users can execute commands or browse through the menus. Usually function keys or key combinations are used as shortcuts.

Assign a single key for frequently performed, small-scale tasks. Assign SHIFT+key combinations for actions that extend or are complementary to the actions of the key or key combination without the SHIFT key. Assign CTRL+key combinations for infrequent actions. Use ALT+letter combinations as mnemonic access characters for menus and dialog boxes. Suggested shortcuts (for the English keyboard) are:

- CTRL+N   New
- CTRL+O   Open
- CTRL+P   Print
- CTRL+S   Save

Recommended shortcuts for MS Windows are:

- CTRL+Z   Undo
- CTRL+X   Cut
- CTRL+C   Copy
- CTRL+V   Paste

Recommended PC function keys assignments are:

- F1 Help
- F6 Move clockwise to next pane of active window
- F8 Toggle extend mode, if supported
- F10 Toggle menu bar activation

The ESC key is generally used to terminate a function or as a default cancel command.

3.3.1.2 Navigation Keys

By pressing the navigation keys, users move the selection cursor around the active window. The navigation keys are: HOME (beginning of line), END (end of line), PAGE UP (screen up), PAGE DOWN (screen down), LEFT ARROW (left one unit), RIGHT ARROW (right one unit), UP ARROW (up one unit), DOWN ARROW (down one unit) TAB (next field).

3.3.2 Mouse Interaction

A mouse is the pointing device used most often in a GUI environment. It can have one, two or three buttons. In a one-button mouse, the button is used for selection. In a two-button mouse, the right button is used for drop-down menu in Windows 95 and NT, and could be used for cancel in MS Windows; left button is used for selection in both. In a three-button mouse, left and middle buttons are used as in a two-button mouse and the right button is free (can be used in application).

Users can move the mouse pointer anywhere on the screen. In mouse based navigation, the pointer tracks the motion of the pointing device. Many recent systems allow developers to define actions that will occur when the mouse navigates within the screens and over or into widgets. Provide "bubble" or "float-over" help facilities for icons and important buttons, with meaningful "hints" at the bottom of the screens, in the message or status line, to guide the user.

Typical mouse selection techniques are the following:

- Click   Selects the choice

  De-selects all other choices

  Sets the anchor point (position from which the selection is extended)

- Shift+Click Selects all choices from the anchor point to the selected choice

  De-selects all other choices

  Preserves the anchor point

- Ctrl+Click   Toggles selection state of the choice

  Preserves selection state of all other choices

  Sets the anchor point

- Ctrl+Shift+Click   Toggles all choices from the anchor point to the selected choice

  Preserves selection state of all other choices

  Preserves the anchor point

Selecting elements from the collection using the mouse is done by clicking, releasing or dragging. Selecting elements from keyboard is done by setting the appropriate mode (normal, add or extended) and then navigating through the collection and selecting.

3.3.2.1 Click

Click is the method of selecting objects and actions. Clicking the mouse button once without pressing any modifier keys, selects a single choice and de-selects all previously selected choices.

3.3.2.2 Double Click

When a 'double-click' is performed on an object that has an implied action, the default action is performed. Do not assign double-click functions to choices on which users will typically perform multiple single clicks, such as on scroll bar buttons.

3.3.3 Actions

Actions are implemented through menus, menu bars, scroll bars and controls. Consistency of similar actions is important in building and reinforcing the users conceptual model. For example, even though text editing and drawing applications are quite different, they both may require that users have the ability to save and retrieve files.

3.3.3.1 Menus

Menus provide users with a list of all available commands. In this way users do not have to remember the syntax for each command. An application can implement three types of menus:

- Pull-down (also known as drop-down),

- Pop-up (also known as contextual),

- Cascading (also known as hierarchical).

For the main application, and any other, menu should be the contemporary windows pull-down menu with a toolbar. The icons on the toolbar will directly correspond to the menu options for each of the commands or functions (eg. as in a Microsoft MDI type menu). A cascading menu may be used as part of the pull-down menu structure where functionally related commands can be structured in a hierarchy.

PanCredit will implement an additional menu structure, which closely resembles the Windows 95 Explorer hierarchy, and where the screen is split into two. The left side has the hierarchy of command options, and the right side is again split into two - the upper half containing a list of the top 10 screen/function names (by user preference), and the bottom a description. This hierarchy menu for the main application will be optional, and GMAC/BIM will easily be able to switch this facility off (as the pull-down menu is the preferred option).

The following guidelines should be used when organising menu items:

- Use ordinary language, not jargon or abbreviations, communicate the actual action to be performed,

- Group related commands together,

- Distinguish between similar commands such as Find and Search with Find File and Search String.

Entries will not be included in menus if they are never available because of window usage constraints or security constraints. If the option is sometimes available but is temporarily unavailable due to window context, it should be *greyed out.*

The following are examples of menus that may be used in a typical application for consistency. It is necessary to provide the menu options for at least Edit, Help, and Print, as these are common and used most.

3.3.3.1.1 Pull-Down Menu

Pull-down menus are the most common type of menus in current applications. These menus contain choices that are related to one another in some manner. For example, all choices in a selected pull-down menu could apply to an entire or selected object, Help information or a view of an object. Provide a pull-down menu for each choice on a menu bar and for the system menu. In creating pull-down menus follow these guidelines:

- Place the most commonly used choices near the top whenever possible,

- Show functionally related choices in logical groups separated by solid lines,

- Do not list more than eight items in a menu; use secondary windows if necessary,

- For choices that result in a dialog box or secondary window, place an ellipsis (...) following the choice,

- For frequently used pull-down choices provide an accelerator,

- Use a plus sign (+) to indicate that users must press two or more keys at the same time.

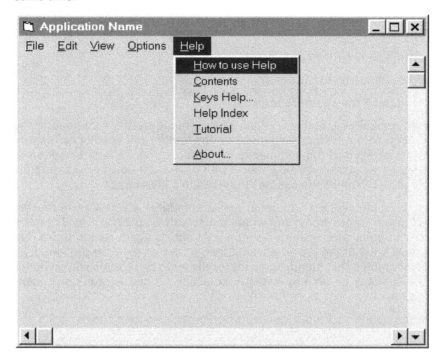

FIGURE 3.3.3.1.1 - WINDOWS PULL-DOWN MENU (HELP MENU)

3.3.3.1.2 Menu Bars

The choices on the menu bar should not be numbered. Use single-word choices. Capitalise only the first letter of a choice unless it contains an acronym, abbreviation or proper noun that is normally capitalised. Each menu bar should have a unique single-character mnemonics for selection (mnemonic access). Mnemonic access is usually underscored.

If the application supports File and Edit, they should be the first two choices on the menu bar. If Help is included in the application, it should always be the last choice on the menu bar. File, Edit and Help pull-down menus can be standardised (text for the pull-down, underscored mnemonics, accelerators); View, Options and Window are recommended.

3.3.3.1.3 Cascading Menu

Cascading does arranging multiple-document interface windows. This technique may be used when many actions can be grouped in related groups or when they are hierarchical in nature. Use a cascaded menu also to reduce the length of a menu.

For example, place a related set of choices in a cascaded menu rather than placing them individually on a pull-down menu. Although the system supports the ability to nest cascaded pull-down menus, the number of menus should be limited. A right-point triangle appears at the right of the pull-down choice text as a visual cue that the choice has an associated pull-down.

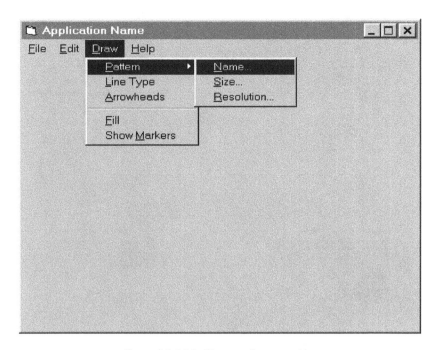

FIGURE 3.3.3.1.3 - WINDOWS CASCADING MENU

3.3.3.1.4 System Menu

Every movable window contains a System menu (also called control menu). The system menu icon is available in the title bar of all windows to provide access to the actions that users can perform on a window, such as moving or sizing. Following are the system menu pull-down actions:

• **Restore** turns the primary window to the size and position it was prior to the last Maximise or Minimise action,

• **Move** allows users to reposition a window,

• **Size** allows users to change the dimensions of a window,

• **Minimise** removes from the screen all windows associated with the active application and places an application icon on the screen,

• **Maximise** enlarges the window to the largest possible size of the screen,

• **Close** removes the window and all associated windows from the screen. The application must be able to recognise potential lost data due to unsaved changes and display a warning message before closing,

• **Switch to** causes the appearance of a dialog box with active applications.

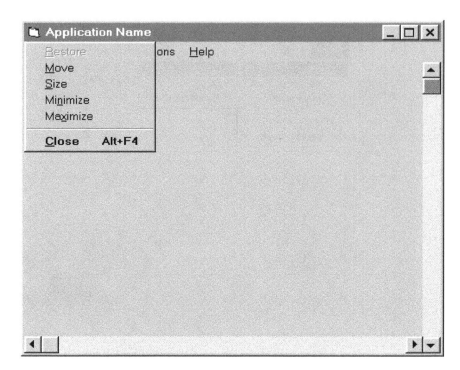

FIGURE 3.3.3.1.4 - WINDOWS CONTROL MENU

3.3.3.1.5 File Pull-Down Menu

Every application that manipulates files as single objects must provide the File Pull Down Menu. The file actions are grouped by task: selecting and saving actions and output actions. In MS Windows and Windows 95 single lines separate groups. Open follows with an ellipsis, which means this action opens a new dialogue box. Provide a Save choice for each object that is not automatically saved when changed. An application should prompt the user for the file name to be used for the save. Exit (optional and a separate group) ends an application and removes from the screen all windows associated with that application. If the application does not have a File Pull-Down menu then Exit should be the last choice on the first pull down menu that is available.

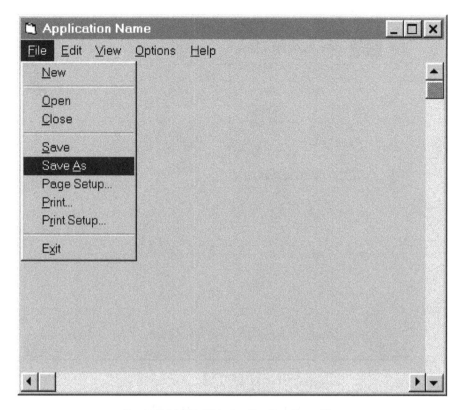

FIGURE 3.3.3.1.5 - WINDOWS FILE PULL-DOWN MENU

3.3.3.1.6 Edit Pull-Down Menu

The Edit actions are grouped into: undo action, clipboard actions and non-clipboard actions. Provide the Edit menu when a menu bar is provided in a window and at least two of the following choices are provided: Undo, Cut, Copy and Paste.

Cut, Copy, Paste and Paste Link are clipboard group actions. Text applications usually compress the space, while graphics drawing applications usually leave the space blank. Paste Link and Links are optional. They are used with Object-Linking and Embedding (OLE - see Section 5). Paste Link creates in the current document a link to an item previously marked in a source document. Links displays the links dialog for changing link properties.

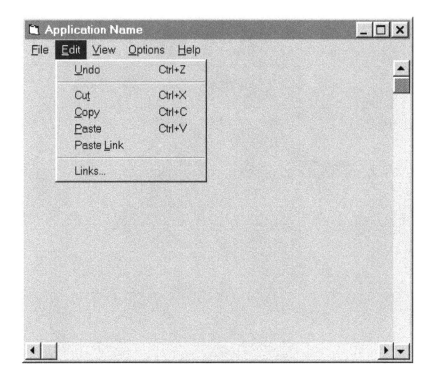

FIGURE 3.3.3.1.6 - WINDOWS EDIT MENU

3.3.3.1.7 View Pull-Down Menu

A view is a way of looking at an object's information. Different views display information in different forms, which mimics the way information is presented in the real world. The View pull-down menu allows users to select different ways to look at the object without affecting the object itself. Provide a View choice on the menu bar of each window that provides a menu bar when more than one view is available for an object. The content of the View pull-down is very specific to the type of object being handled by application. Therefore, the View pull-down cannot be standardised.

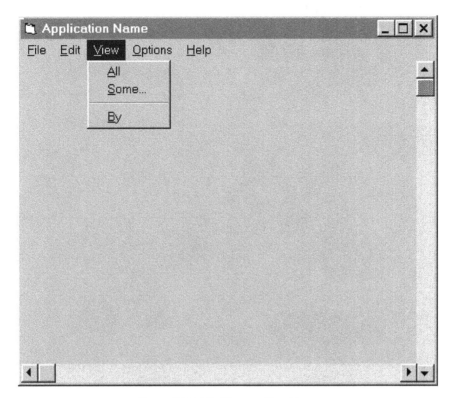

FIGURE 3.3.3.1.7 – WINDOWS VIEW MENU

3.3.3.1.8 Tools Pull-Down Menu

While the View pull-down menu provides a means for users to customise the appearance of a user object, the Options pull-down menu provides a means for users to customise the application object. Provide an Options choice on the menu bar in each window that provides a menu bar and where a user will be able to tailor the appearance or behaviour of the product. The Options pull-down is also very specific to a particular application so its contents cannot be standardised.

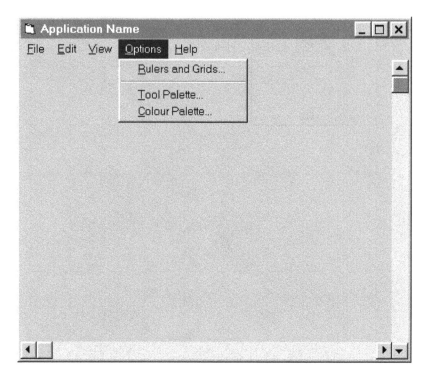

FIGURE 3.3.3.1.8 - WINDOWS OPTIONS MENU

3.3.3.1.9 Window Pull-Down Menu

The ability to open multiple document windows adds a requirement for an additional menu bar command that manipulates document windows. It is also very specific to a particular application so its contents cannot be standardised.

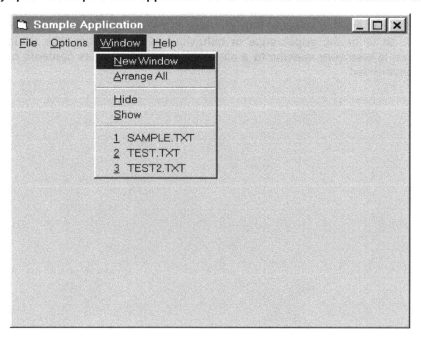

FIGURE 3.3.3.1.9 – WINDOWS WINDOW MENU

3.3.3.1.10 Help Pull-Down Menu

While running an application, users occasionally require additional information. The main purpose of Help is to provide online assistance, not to tutor users. Users can request help by pressing the F1 key, selecting the Help push button or choosing the help action from the Help pull-down menu. Following are types of help:

- Contextual Help   specific information about the item which is selected,

- Help for help   information on how to use help facility,

- Keys help   key assignments of an application,

- Help index an alphabetic list of all the help index entries,

- Tutorial (optional) provides access to a tutorial, if applicable,

- Version (About)   information about the application,

The Help window title must present the title of an application followed by Help. A help window should be placed, if possible, where it is completely visible on the screen and does not overlay any of the application windows.

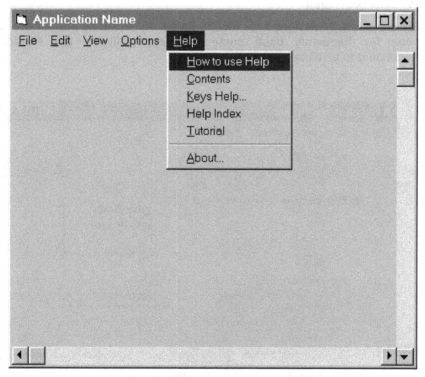

FIGURE 3.3.3.1.10 - WINDOWS HELP MENU

Here are some guidelines in designing effective user help:

- Describe a task, not the computer's representation,

- Use an active voice,

- Make it easily accessible,

- Make it easily removable from the screen,

- Do not ignore a plea for help; a response "No help is available" is better than no response at all,

- Refer the user to the documentation or another detailed description,

- Allow the user to navigate through Help. This will be developed using the Microsoft Help Compiler, where the text will be written in Rich-Text Format,

- Do not state the obvious,

- Provide the users with the ability to jump from one topic to another; keep track of topics so that the users can go back to the previous topic,

- Allow the use of bookmarks that enable users to go to frequently used topics.

3.3.3.1.11 Pop-Up Menu

Pop-up menus contain only those choices that are valid for an object at the time the menu is displayed. The menus are called pop-up menus because they appear to "pop up" next to an object when specifically invoked by the user. Pop-up menus are designed to provide an efficient method for accessing common, contextual commands.

They are primarily designed for mouse users. Applications should use pop-up menus for frequently used commands, especially in the Windows 95 environment to be consistent.

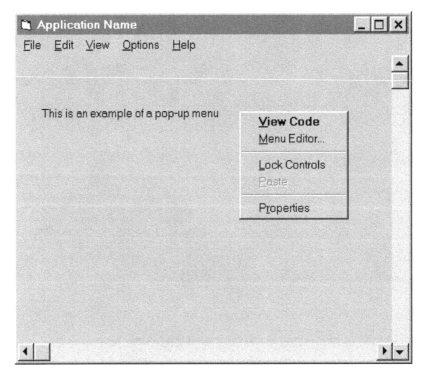

FIGURE 3.3.3.1.11 - WINDOWS POP-UP MENU

3.3.3.2 Controls

A control is an interface component that enables users to select choices and type or see information. The most common GUI controls, referred to also as widgets and items depending on the vendor of the development tool, are:

- Spin button,

- Table/Grid/Array Field,

- Outline Field,

- Push button,

- List box,

- Combination box,

- Drop-down combination box,

- Drop-down list,

- Tool Palette,

- Label,

- Radio button,

- Check box,

- Text/Entry field and Rich Text Control,

- VBX control and OLE Container,

- Image Control,

- Tab Folders,

- List Of Values.

3.3.3.2.1 Spin Button

A spin button allows users to complete an entry field by scrolling through an incremental or decremented scale of choices. Use a spin button to display a list of choices that have a logical consecutive order. For example, use a spin button for a list of the months or dates of the year. When a list of choices does not have a logical consecutive order, use a drop-down list or drop-down combination box. When you first display a spin button, it must contain a default choice.

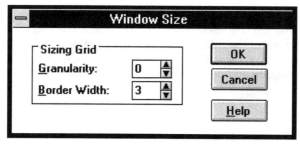

FIGURE 3.3.3.2.1 - SPIN BUTTON

3.3.3.2.2 Table/Grid/Array Fields

Tables and grids make it easier for the user to view and manipulate records. These must be used in activities where there are one-to-many relationships between types of information. Columns should be wide enough for the maximum possible width of the data of the field - this will usually be known from the data specification (or see the database administrator). For wide columns allow scrolling. To move the cursor from column to column, use the TAB, or RETURN keys.

Product	Price	Stocked	Dropped
Dharamsala Tea	18.00	150	Yes
Tibetan Barley Beer	19.00	2000	No
Licorice Syrup	5.00	610	No
Chef Anton's Seaso	14.00	480	
Chef Anton's Gumbo	11.00	900	
Tomato Soup X	4.00	1200	

FIGURE 3.3.3.2.2/1 - GRID EXAMPLE WITH SCROLL-BAR

Array field is an array of any of the screen controls, most commonly DataFields. This type of window will be used to show multiple records where there is a requirement to edit the records actually in the grid. Each column in the array has its own label defined in the ArrayField. ArrayFields should automatically resize when the window is resized.

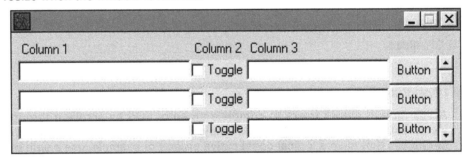

FIGURE 3.3.3.2.2/2 - ARRAY FIELD

3.3.3.2.3 Outline Fields

Outline fields can be extremely useful for displaying data. They can display hierarchies and can be easily resized. Their main drawback is that data cannot be directly entered or edited into the field, it has to be manipulated via a separate dialog box. As such, Outline fields are useful for displaying result sets that will not require editing in place.

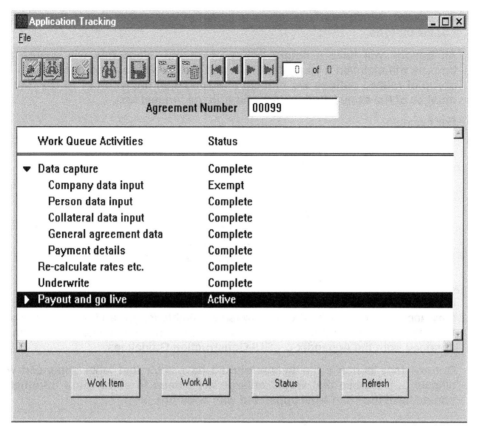

Figure 3.3.3.2.3 - Outline Field

3.3.3.2.4 Command Button

Command buttons (or Push buttons) should display available actions that are not available for invocation through the menu bar, especially in dialog boxes, message boxes, and some secondary windows. When the user presses the button, an action occurs immediately. Use push button names that are self-explanatory. For push buttons that open up another dialog box, the dialog box title should match the push button name. Decide on the largest text that will be required as the label within the push button, and all buttons must be consistent in size within the application.

It is also possible to invoke other modal or modeless screens by clicking on a command button, but this should be avoided in order to maintain simplicity and reduce development complexity.

FIGURE 3.3.3.2.4/1 - COMMAND BUTTON

For a row of buttons, always locate the OK button at the far left, followed by the Cancel button. The Help button should be at the far right with custom buttons in between. Windows where data manipulation is possible should have OK and Cancel buttons.

All buttons will have a height policy of natural, since this will ensure that buttons will maintain a consistent look and feel throughout the application. If a group of related buttons are present in a row, then the width of all the buttons must be of the same length as the one with the longest text.

For example:

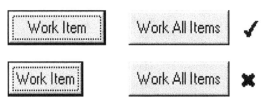

FIGURE 3.3.3.2.4/2 - CONSISTENT COMMAND BUTTONS

If the button text is excessive and would create an unacceptably long button (say, more than 1.5 inches) then choose a suitable length and truncate the text. Further details of button dimensions and related screen geography can be obtained from the Appendix D - GUI Construction Guidelines.

Buttons that launch a dialog box should have their test label appended with ellipsis (...). Those that would enlarge the screen to show more information should have their text label appended with chevrons (>>).

3.3.3.2.5 List Box

A list box is a rectangular box with scroll bars that usually contains a scrollable list of choices from which users can select one. Use a list box to display a list of settings choices where screen space is not a limiting factor, in which the number of choices may vary. List box choices should be in alphabetical order or any other logical order. List boxes should typically display only 6 to 8 choices at one time. List box headings should be positioned above the list box, left-aligned.

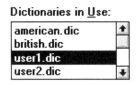

FIGURE 3.3.3.2.5 - LIST BOX

3.3.3.2.6 Combination Boxes

A combination box is a control that combines the capabilities of both an entry field and a list box. The list box appears beneath and to the right of an entry field. Provide a combination box when a user may have to type values that cannot be provided by the product and a set of commonly used choices can be provided.

They should be used where the list of data options is more than 15 and less than 100 items. Where there are more than 100 entries in a list, a simple search screen should be used. Where possible, items should be held in alphabetical sequence, so that the user knows whether to scroll up or down. On entry the most commonly used option should be selected as default, rather than the first item on the list.

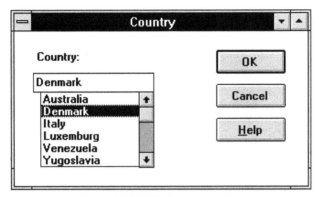

FIGURE 3.3.3.2.6/1 - COMBINATION BOX

A drop-down combination box is a variation of the combination box in which the list box is hidden until users request it. Users see a prompt box containing a downward-pointing arrow at the right side of an entry field. Use drop-down combination boxes when presentation space is limited (not enough space to use a combination box), or when the user will complete an entry field more often by typing text than by choosing the entry field from a list.

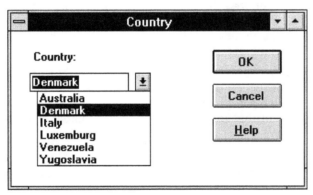

FIGURE 3.3.3.2.6/2 - DROP-DOWN COMBINATION BOX

3.3.3.2.7 Drop-Down List

A drop-down list is similar to a drop-down combination box, but instead of an entry field for typing text it has a single selection field with one choice displayed as the default value. Use a drop-down list when a choice or object is not changed frequently or when space is so limited that the window does not have enough space to display a list box.

Drop-down List Boxes should only be used where a user is to select from a finite list of 15 values or less. A List of Values control should be used for lists of more than 15 items.

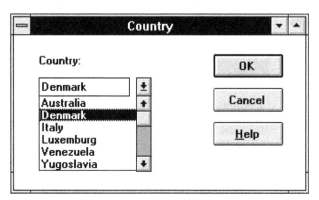

FIGURE 3.3.3.2.7 - DROP-DOWN LIST

3.3.3.2.8 Tool Palette/Tool Bar and Tool-tips

One or more controls in a window or menu that provide a set of graphical choices that represent tools is called a tool palette or tool bar. A tool bar must be developed to provide the user with a quick route to executing helpful and repetitive functions, e.g. print, save help, etc.

Iconic buttons to invoke other functions or forms from the current form will be placed on the toolbar. So, for instance, if the user wishes to enter comments for a customer, an icon would be enabled on the toolbar. Icons will not be embedded on a form. Only buttons will be used on forms.

ToolTips, also referred to as bubble-help or float-over-help, are yellow rectangles that display the name or short description of a tool bar button when the user rests the mouse pointer over the button. The tool tip for the button disappears when the user navigates off the button.

In theory, tool-tips can be present on any control but generally they are used only for controls, which do not have text labels. Tool-tips should consist of a short descriptive piece of text, preferably less than four words. The text should identify the action that is expected when the toolbar button/Picture-Button is pressed.

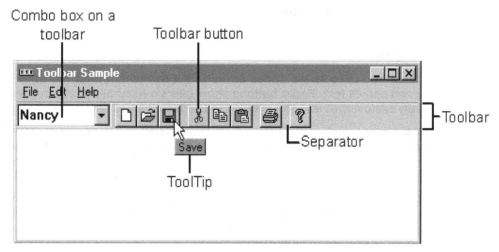

FIGURE 3.3.3.2.8 - TOOL PALETTE

3.3.3.2.9 Label

A label or field prompt is descriptive, static, text for entry fields. It must be positioned above or to the left of the field.

Labels located above a field should be left-aligned with the beginning of the field. A label located to the left of a field should be left-aligned with other labels. Capitalise only the first letter of the first word unless one of the other words is normally capitalised. Column heading labels should be justified in the same way as the data it pertains to. If the group is separated by a group box, the label/title should appear inside the top left-hand corner of the box.

Use descriptive text on the message bar, or field of controls, to provide additional information about a control, when other labels are not sufficient to explain its function. For example, describe the required date format for an entry field that will contain a date, or use messages in the status bar.

FIGURE 3.3.3.2.9 USAGE OF FONTS IN LABELS

TextGraphic (Boiler Plate text in Oracle Forms or Uniface) must be used for labels.

*   All monetary fields should have template of CURRENCY,

*   All numeric fields should be right-justified,

*   All date fields should have template of DATE,

- All label text will be in UK English.

3.3.3.2.10 Radio Button

A radio button (also called option button), is a two-part control consisting of a circle and choice text. Radio buttons show users a fixed set of choices that are mutually exclusive (it is recommended to use less than 10 choices if possible).

When the user selects a radio button, its circle is partially filled. When more than one object is selected, a situation can occur in which the current state cannot be reflected by one radio button (for example a part of selected text can be bold or underlined). In that situation, all radio buttons in the group should be off.

Place the radio buttons in the order the user would logically walk through. Use default actions in radio buttons by already having a button selected. The default radio button should be the first radio button in the group. Option Buttons should never be used in multi-record blocks.

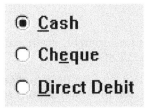

FIGURE 3.3.3.2.10 - RADIO BUTTONS

3.3.3.2.11 Check Box

A check box is a two-part control consisting of a square box and choice text. A check box acts like a switch. Unlike radio buttons, check boxes are not mutually exclusive. Use a check box to display individual settings choice that can be set to on or off. When users select a check box, its square box is filled with X. When more than one object is selected, a situation can occur in which the current state of a check box is neither completely on, nor off (for example a part of selected text can be bold or underlined). When this happens, the square box in MS Windows is filled with grey. Force only one state, either checked or unchecked.

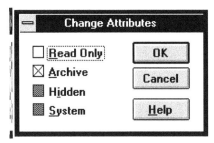

FIGURE 3.3.3.2.11 - CHECK BOX

3.3.3.2.12 Text/Entry Field and Rich Text Control

In entry field or text box is a rectangular box into which users type information. Provide an entry field to allow a user to type values that cannot be supplied by the product as a list of choices, or for entering comments. Character entry fields should be left justified, integer and float entry fields right justified. Information can be limited to one line (single-line entry field) or it can have more than one line (multiple-line entry field) - in this case the rich-edit facility should be used with the Notepad look as default.

Entry fields should be wide enough to accommodate the largest possible value and account for expandable fonts; use widest letter "W" to determine the maximum width. You can provide horizontal scrolling for the text that exceeds the length. Do not use scrollable entry fields for information that is short or fixed in length, such as date or time. Sample data, such as 9999.99, should not be displayed.

Tab and Enter keys are used to move the cursor between fields and to perform the default action, respectively. Tab stop should be assigned to every user input field; the tabbing sequence should be left-to-right, and from top-to-bottom. In multiple-line entry fields Tab and Enter are also traditionally used for moving the cursor to the next tab stop or next line.

Entry fields support two modes, insert and replace. In insert mode, the character is inserted where the cursor position is. In replace mode, the selected text is deleted and the typed character is inserted in its place. Users toggle between the two modes using Insert (Ins) key. When the field is in update (insert/replace) mode the field colour must be white, and grey when in enquiry mode.

Some values contain dashes, slashes or other characters that can be either advance defined or user defined. The user should be able to enter values either with (masked) or without (unmasked) these characters. The value must be automatically masked by the system.

Text boxes used simply for the display of information should have the 3D indented look but should adopt the inactive background colour whilst retaining the active foreground colour. With default attributes, this will result in black (not grey) text in a 3D box with a grey background. The purpose of this is to make the differentiation between labels and data more clear.

Note that this approach deviates from Microsoft standards, which differ only in that the 3D box is omitted.

An illustration of text fields and how they must appear is given in figure 3.3.3.2.9.

A rich edit control is a window in which a user can both enter and edit text. Just as a multi-line edit control provides a programming interface for entering and editing multiple lines of text, a rich edit control provides a programming interface for formatting text. A user can assign both character and paragraph formatting (making words boldface or italic, adding underlining, or realigning paragraphs, for instance) and can include embedded OLE objects in the text.

Rich edit controls are based on multi-line edit controls, and they support almost all the messages and notifications used with multi-line edit controls.

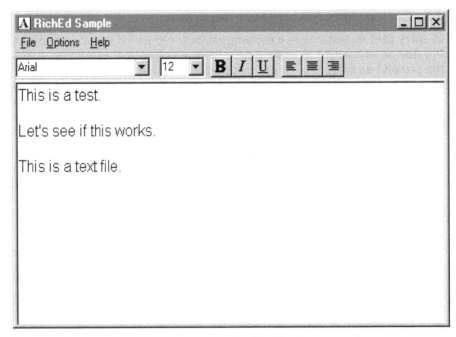

FIGURE 3.3.3.2.12 - RICH-EDIT TEXT BOX

3.3.3.2.13 VBX Control and OLE Container

This can be included in the form module by creating a custom item and setting the relevant properties. The size and the usage characteristics (of the VBX or OCX), will be determined by the type of VBX, project requirements and the vendor's recommendations. Ensure that the VBX is fully compatible with the development tool, which will use it.

For 32-bit applications, i.e. those running on Windows 95 or Windows NT, OCX controls will be used. These will be third party add-ons to the GUI development tool; Visual Basic 4 already caters for this.

OLE containers provide a way of accessing other Windows applications through either linking or embedding, e.g. Microsoft Word, Excel, etc.

3.3.3.2.14 Image Control

The Image Control displays bitmaps, icons, or Windows metafiles, acts like a command button when clicked. Supported file types are PCX, TIFF, JFIF, PICT, PCD, CALS, GIF, BMP and RAS. Use the image item on an as-needed basis, e.g. document imaging, or other specific applications. Keep image sizes as small as possible without compromising visible detail, in order to establish good performance.

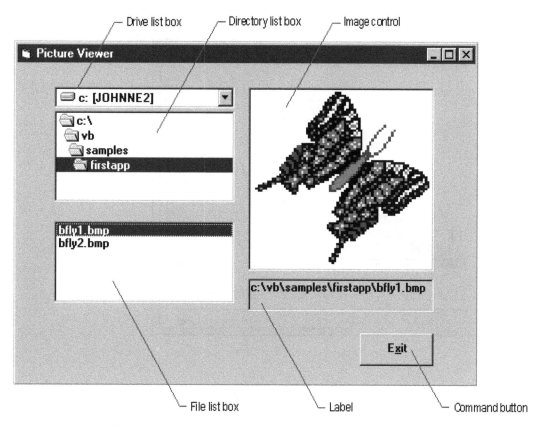

FIGURE 3.3.3.2.14 - IMAGE CONTROL USED FOR PICTURE VIEWER

3.3.3.2.15 Tab Folders

Tab folders or cards are layers of superimposed sections within the same screen. Use this feature where the development tool permits. Clicking on the relevant flap, which is appropriately text-headed, can access each tab folder. Tab folders are used in favour of separate screens in order to accommodate as much information and processing as possible in one logical business process.

Tab

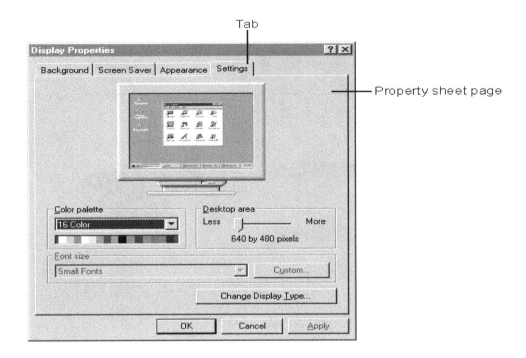

Property sheet page

FIGURE 3.3.3.2.15 - TAB FOLDERS

Where Tab folder functionality is not readily available, specifically where much effort would be required for complex functionality, use should be made of the specified VBX, which will enable Microsoft-type Tab folders to be developed. Development of Tab folders is, however, possible but the relative effort required is higher. The individual Tabs must first be developed as individual window objects, then they are enveloped into one window with many Tabs folders.

Do not have more than 8 Tabs in one window. The area occupied by the tab folders can vary, but it is recommended to allow enough space with respect to all other fields on the screen for better presentation - typically tab folders occupy the bottom ¾ of the screen. The top ¼ of the screen may be used for displaying generic record information, such as contract number, name, etc.

3.3.3.2.16 List of Values

Where new, as well as existing entries, need to be viewed or entered, the concept of a List of Values should be used. In this case, an icon indicates that a List of Values is available. When double-clicked, a secondary window should be displayed that will allow the user to search for existing entries. Alternatively, a *New* button should be used to add new entries to the list.

The List Of Values feature is better implemented using Scaffolds. There will be two types of List of Values screens, as follows:

• Simple - this type consists of only one searchable column, usually a description of some type. A Text Field will allow data entry and an Outline Field (result set), positioned directly below, will scroll to the matching entry.

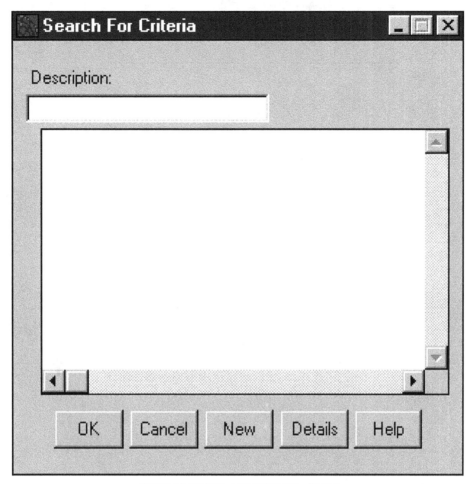

FIGURE 3.3.3.2.16/1 - LIST OF VALUES – SIMPLE

- **Complex - this type is needed where there will be more than one column used for a search. For example, when locating a customer a user may want to use the surname, forenames, address or other criteria as search filters. Text Fields will be provided for each search filter and the Outline Field will only be populated when the user acknowledges that enough search criteria have been entered and the search is executed.**

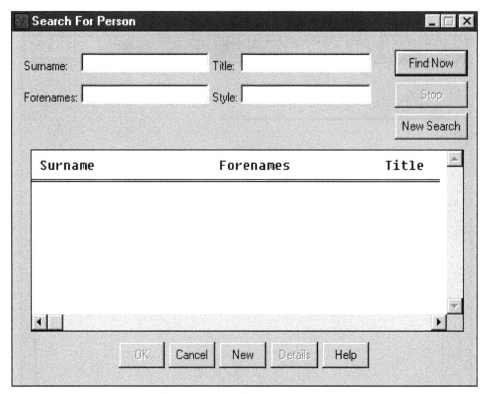

FIGURE 3.3.3.2.16/2 - LIST OF VALUES – COMPLEX

3.3.3.3 Scroll Bars

A scroll bar consists of a scroll area with a slider box inside and an arrow at each end. A window can have either a vertical or horizontal scroll bar or both. A vertical scroll bar appears on the right side of a window; a horizontal scroll bar appears at the bottom of a window. A horizontal scroll bar should be at least half the width of the scrollable portion of the client area.

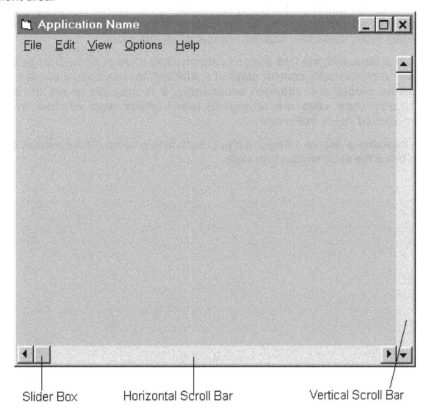

FIGURE 3.3.3.3 - SCROLL BARS

The slider box represents the position of the visible information in relation to all the information that is available. The scroll bar arrows show users the direction of scrolling. Whenever the size of the window changes, the components must reflect the new state.

You should use scroll bars in all sizeable windows when the object contained in the window will not be completely displayed. If the size of the window is reduced, scroll bars should automatically be displayed. If your application has a choice of presenting information from top-to-bottom or left-to-right, you should present the scrollable information from top-to-bottom. Users find it easier to move in a vertical direction.

Users can scroll information using either the mouse or the keyboard. Scrolling can be incremental (by clicking on the scroll bar arrow or pressing the arrow keys), by page (a click above or below the slider box in scroll area or pressing PgUp and PgDn keys scrolls vertically one page; a click left or right from the slider box or Ctrl+PgUp and Ctrl+PgDn keys scrolls horizontally) or direct positioning (by dragging the slider box in the scroll area).

3.3.3.4 Compound Widgets

The widgets can be grouped and manipulated together. Compound widgets are of four types:

- Panel - allows grouping of widgets into discrete areas or functional groups on the window, which can be treated as a separate units.

- Array field - displays a group of widgets in tabular form, and the top widget in each column becomes the template field for the column in the array field. It is possible to set the column titles, scroll bar, and the number of visible rows.

- Grid field – it groups widgets into aligned columns and rows of cells. Grid fields can also be used to dynamically control parts of a window; for example, a section of the window can be hidden and adjusted accordingly. It is possible to set the default margins, gravity (how cells are arranged), insert policy, and whether invisible widgets are allotted space in the grid.

- Viewport - contains a view to a larger widget, such as a graphic. The viewport can be scrolled to bring the child widget into view.

4.0 MULTIMEDIA DESIGN

A multimedia user interface allows a user to work with more complex types of information, such as synchronised audio and video information. In addition to text and simple graphics, a multimedia user interface typically uses:

- Images, both static and moving, recorded and synthesised,

- Audio, both recorded and synthesised.

4.1 MULTIMEDIA INTERFACE

A multimedia interface can include:

- Enhanced visible cues, such as animated icons,

- Enhanced audible cues, such as speech or music,

- Animated objects, such as charts and graphs,

- Video images, such as product demonstrations,

- Computer visualisations, such as images based on data gathered from sensors.

4.2 DESIGN CONSIDERATIONS

A designer can use standard components of the GUI, such as windows and controls, to display a multimedia object. For example, a product could display the wave form for an audio signal in a window.

A designer can modify the visuals for controls when appropriate. For example, in a product used for video recording, the push buttons could be designed to resemble the Record, Pause, and Play buttons on an actual video recorder.

Factors that affect a user's ability to manage and manipulate multimedia objects include:

- Size, Colour, and resolution of a user's display screen,

- Adapter cards and peripheral hardware, such as video or audio players or recorders,

- System memory and storage capacity.

4.3 MULTIMEDIA OBJECT

A multimedia object is typically a collection of data presented to a user in succession. To be displayed correctly, the data in a multimedia object must be presented to a user in the correct sequence and at the correct time. For example, an animation sequence is presented to a user as a series of images rather than as a single image. For the sequence to play correctly, each frame must appear in the correct relative order, and the interval from the appearance of one frame to the appearance of the next must be constant and must match the interval at which the sequence was developed.

5.0 OBJECT LINKING AND EMBEDDING

Users want to create documents that integrate several types of information (for example spreadsheets, databases, charts) through one GUI, without switching between applications. They want a consistent way to manipulate information without dealing with different interfaces.

Different types of information can be integrated using the concept of compound documents. A compound document is a container that includes components from various sources. In compound documents the user can insert text, a table, a picture or a chart. The container always invokes an application that can handle particular information (for example spreadsheet application for a spreadsheet). Thus, users can manipulate various types of information within the body of the single document. They can create a single document that either links or embeds different objects. Object Linking and Embedding (OLE) is the process of creating compound documents that contain embedded and linked objects.

5.1 OLE CONCEPTS

OLE Concepts are:

- Object   An object is an information entity (for example text, graphics, sound),

- Class   The object class describes the type of information

  (For example picture or chart),

- Client   Client is the application that produces a container document,

- Server   Server is the application that produces the embedded or linked document,

- Package   A package contains OLE object, a file or a command line. Double-clicking a package object activates the object inside the package,

- Embedding   Embedding is the process of inserting an object into a container document,

- Linking   In linking an object it appears inside the container as if it had been physically copied; in fact, the container simply contains a link.

5.2 OLE INTERFACE

The OLE interface provides easy methods for inserting, editing, viewing and activating linked and embedded objects. The OLE process requires a dialog between client and server. Any application can be a client, a server or both. Clients have four commands added to the Edit menu (see Edit pull-down menu): Paste Special (and/or Paste Link), Links, Object and Insert Object (last two are optional). In server, the File menu is modified: Save command should be replaced by Update; Close command should be replaced by Close & Return; Save As, command should be replaced by Save Copy As, and finally Exit command should be replaced by Exit & Return to.

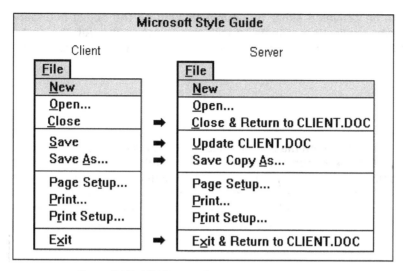

FIGURE 5.2/1 - MS WINDOWS SERVER INTERFACE CHANGES

In word-processing applications like Word, inserting linked and embedded objects can be done through Cut, Copy and Paste, and Paste Special and/or Paste Link (for inserting linked objects) commands on the Edit menu or through Insert Object command that application should support. Copying linked objects is done through Copy and Paste (not Paste Link).

The user can modify the object with the editing tools provided by the server. For example, when an application functions as a server, the Update command updates the object in the container document, but does not close the server. The Save Copy As command saves a copy of the embedded object in a separate file.

An object in a compound document can be inactive, selected or opened. The application should provide visual indication of object status. In addition visual indication should be different for selected linked and embedded objects, because of different operations on them.

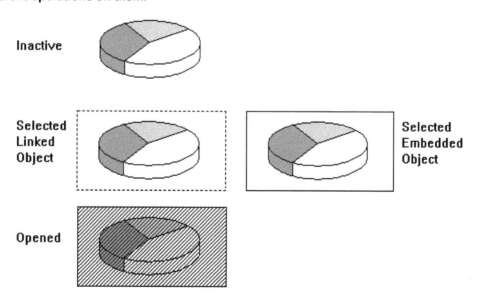

FIGURE 5.2/2 - MS WINDOWS VISUAL APPEARANCE RECOMMENDATIONS

OLE objects can be activated either by double-clicking on the object boundary which invokes the server application associated with the object or through the command in the Edit menu. If the server is busy or unavailable, the warning message should be displayed.

5.3 OLE LINKS

OLE Links relies on dialog with the source document. A Links dialog box should display all links contained in the document. Beside the list, Links dialog box should contain buttons for updating all links selected in the list (Update Now), permanently breaking the link between the client and server (Cancel Link) and a button for changing the link (Change Link). Change link should invoke another dialog box for establishing the link. OK and Cancel are standard buttons for confirming the changes and discarding all changes.

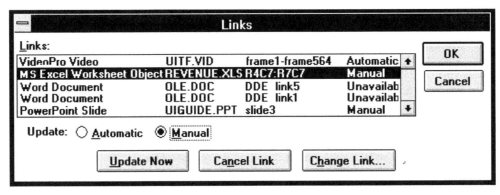

FIGURE 5.3 - MS WINDOWS LINKS DIALOG BOX

GLOSSARY OF TERMS

-B-

Button (command button)   A control that initiates a command or sets an option.

-C-

Check box   A control that displays a setting, either checked (set) or unchecked (not set).

Click   To position the mouse pointer over an object and then press and release a mouse button.

Clipboard   The area of storage for objects, data, or their references, after a user carries out a Cut or Copy command.

Combo-box   A control that combines a text box and interdependent list box.

Container   An object that holds other objects.

Context-sensitive Help   Information about an object and its current condition.

Control   An object that enables user interaction or input, often to initiate an action, display information, or set values.

-D-

Dialog box   A secondary window that gathers additional information from a user. cf. message box

Double-click   To press and release a mouse button twice in rapid succession.

Drag   To press and hold a mouse button while moving the mouse.

Drag and drop   A technique for moving, copying or linking an object by dragging. The destination determines the interpretation of the operation.

Drop-down menu   A menu that is displayed from a menu bar.

-E-

Event   An action or occurrence to which an application can respond. Examples of events are clicks, key presses, and mouse movements.

-G-

Greyed   The state of a control whose normal functionality is not presently available to a user.

Group box   A control that groups a set of controls.

-I-

Icon   A pictorial representation of an object.

Inactive window   A window in which a user's input is not currently being directed. An inactive window is typically distinguished by the colour of its title bar.

Input focus   The location where the user is currently directing input.

-L-

Label (caption)	The text (or graphic) that identifies a control.

-M-

Maximise	To make a window its largest size.
MDI	Multiple document interface. A technique for managing a set of windows whereby documents are opened into windows that are constrained to a single primary window.
Menu bar	A horizontal bar at the top of a window, below the title bar, that contains menus.
Message box	A secondary window that is displayed to inform a user about a particular condition. cf. dialog box.
Minimize	To minimise the size of a window (i.e. reduce it to an icon).
Modal	A restrictive or limiting interaction because of operating in a mode. Modal often describes a secondary window that restricts a user's interaction with other windows. A secondary window can be modal with respect to its primary window or to the entire system. cf. modeless.
Modeless	Not restrictive or limiting interaction. Modeless often describes a secondary window that does not restrict a user's interaction with other windows. cf. modal.

-O-

Object	An entity or component identifiable by a user that can be distinguished by its properties, operations and relationships.

-P-

Point	To position the pointer over a particular object and location.
Poplist (drop-down list)	A control that displays a current setting, but can be opened to display a list of choices.
Properties	Attributes or characteristics of an object that define its state, appearance or value.

-R-

Radio button	A control that allows a user to select from a fixed set of mutually exclusive choices.

-S-

Scroll	To move the view of an object or information to make a different portion visible.
Scroll bar	A control that supports scrolling.
Shortcut key	A keyboard key or key combination that invokes a particular command.

-T-

Text box	A control in which a user can enter and edit text.
Title bar	The horizontal area at the top of a window that identifies the window.

Toolbar	A frame or special area that contains a set of other controls, e.g. buttons.
Tooltip	A control that provides a small pop-up window that provides descriptive text, such as a label, for a control or graphic object.
-W-	
Window	An object that displays information. A window is a separately controllable area of the screen that typically has a rectangular border.

APPENDICES

APPENDIX 1: VISUAL BASIC GUI CONTROL REFERENCE

As the general GUI development direction within a project is to be consistent with Microsoft Windows look and feel, it is recommended to refer to Microsoft developments and facilities where additional controls and features are required. The Microsoft Press publication titled 'The Windows Interface Guidelines for Software Design' should be referred to when in doubt.

In order to provide a reference (only) of the current Microsoft Visual Basic features, a list of the controls are provided below. These are not exhaustive on the general subject of GUI controls, but are only a Microsoft-based guide to further GUI development. Many features have already been covered in the main document above.

Button Class Name	Description
	Pointer - provides a way to move and resize forms and controls (Note that this is not a control)
	PictureBox - displays bitmaps, icons, or Windows metafiles. It displays text or acts as a visual container for other controls
	Label - displays text a user cannot interact with or modify
	Text box - provides an area to enter or display text
	Frame - provides a visual and functional container for controls
	Command Button - carries out a command or action when a user chooses it
	Check Box - displays a True/False or Yes/No option. You can check any number of check boxes on a form at one time
	Option Button - as part of an option group with other option buttons, displays multiple choices, from which a user can choose only one

Combo Box - combines a text box with a list box. Allows a user to type in a selection or select an item from a drop-down list

List Box - displays a list of items that a user can choose from

Horizontal and Vertical Scroll Bars - allow a user to select a value within a range of values. (These are used as separate controls and are not the same as the built-in scroll bars found with many controls)

Timer - executes timer events at specified time intervals

Drive List Box - displays and allows a user to select valid disk drives

Directory List Box - displays and allows a user to select directories and paths

File List Box - displays and allows a user to select from a list of files

Shape - adds a rectangle, square, ellipse, or circle to a form

Line - adds a straight-line segment to a form

Image - displays bitmaps, icons, or Windows metafiles; acts like a command button when clicked

Data - enables you to connect to an existing database and display information from it on your forms

OLE container - embeds data into a Visual Basic application

DBCombo (data-bound) box - provides most of the features of the standard combo box control, plus increased data access capabilities

 DBGrid (data-bound) - provides most of the features of the standard grid control, plus increased data access capabilities

 DBList (data-bound) box - provides most of the features of the standard list box control, plus increased data access capabilities

 Menu - creates menus in your Visual Basic applications. For information about menu controls, you work with menu controls in the Menu Editor, which you can access either by choosing Menu Editor from the Tools menu, or by clicking the Menu Editor button on the toolbar.

APPENDIX 2: STANDARD VISUAL BASIC CUSTOM CONTROLS

A custom control is an extension to the Visual Basic Toolbox, and is used as any of the standard built-in controls, such as the check box control. For example, the Visual Basic 4 includes as standard custom controls that allow the display of graphs and gauges, view data in a database, and create multimedia applications.

When a custom control is added to the application project, its icon is displayed in the Visual Basic Toolbox. The icons for the custom controls are listed in the following table.

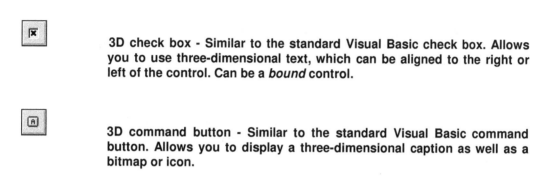

3D check box - Similar to the standard Visual Basic check box. Allows you to use three-dimensional text, which can be aligned to the right or left of the control. Can be a *bound* control.

3D command button - Similar to the standard Visual Basic command button. Allows you to display a three-dimensional caption as well as a bitmap or icon.

3D frame - Emulates the standard Visual Basic frame control. Allows you to display three-dimensional text. The frame itself can be displayed either raised or inset.

3D group push button - Emulates the functionality of the Ribbon in Microsoft Excel spreadsheets or the toolbar in Microsoft Word for Windows word processing program.

3D option button - Similar to the standard Visual Basic option button. Allows the use of three-dimensional text, which can be aligned to the right or left of the control.

3D panel - Displays three-dimensional text on a three-dimensional background, or groups other controls on a three-dimensional background. Can be a *bound* control.

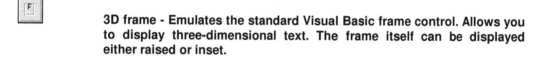

Communications - Provides complete serial communications for your applications. Allows the transmission and reception of data through a serial port.

Graph - Displays many different types and styles of graphs.

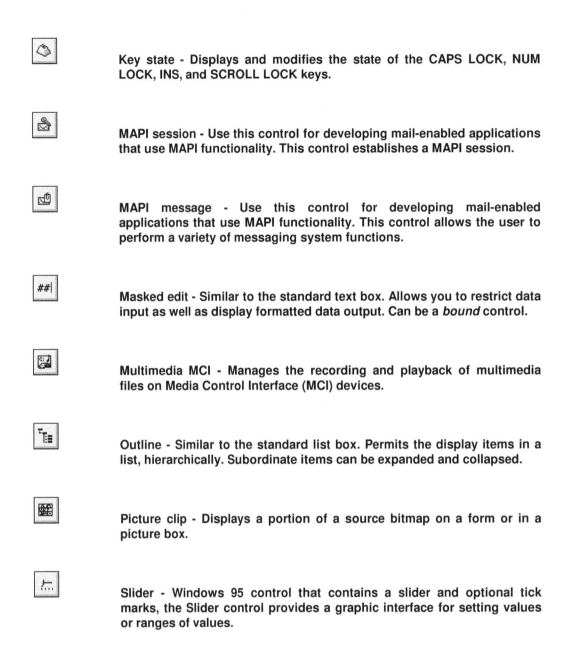

Key state - Displays and modifies the state of the CAPS LOCK, NUM LOCK, INS, and SCROLL LOCK keys.

MAPI session - Use this control for developing mail-enabled applications that use MAPI functionality. This control establishes a MAPI session.

MAPI message - Use this control for developing mail-enabled applications that use MAPI functionality. This control allows the user to perform a variety of messaging system functions.

Masked edit - Similar to the standard text box. Allows you to restrict data input as well as display formatted data output. Can be a *bound* control.

Multimedia MCI - Manages the recording and playback of multimedia files on Media Control Interface (MCI) devices.

Outline - Similar to the standard list box. Permits the display items in a list, hierarchically. Subordinate items can be expanded and collapsed.

Picture clip - Displays a portion of a source bitmap on a form or in a picture box.

Slider - Windows 95 control that contains a slider and optional tick marks, the Slider control provides a graphic interface for setting values or ranges of values.

Index

1. **TITLE:**   THERAPEUTIC PHILOSOPHY FOR THE INDIVIDUAL AND THE STATE

YEAR: 1998

PRICE: £39

ISBN: 0 9527956 5 5

DESCRIPTION: Concepts and didactics of philosophers through the ages. From the Hellenic rhetorics, to recent European schools of ideas. The logic of Therapeutic Philosophy expressed assists in the understanding of human behaviour and the way in which philosophy can contribute to the treatment of the individual and the state.

2. **TITLE:**   PHILOSOPHIC COUNSELLING FOR PEOPLE AND THEIR GOVERNMENTS

YEAR: 1999

PRICE: £19

ISBN: 0 9527956 6 3

DESCRIPTION: The logic of philosophic counselling assists in the understanding of human behaviour and can contribute to the treatment of the people and their governments. Philosophic Counselling has been with us since the times Pericles, the Golden Age of Athens. As such, this book includes the ideas of Plato, Aristotle, Machiavelli, Hobbes, Locke, Rousseau, Hume, Burke, Hegel, Bentham, Mill, Marx and other philosophers in contemporary counselling.

3. **TITLE:**   A TOWN CALLED MORPHOU.

YEAR: 1998

PRICE: £7-50

ISBN: 0 9527956 2 0

DESCRIPTION: The forceful simplicity of the majority of these verses own their existence to the adoration of the opposite sex, freedom, patriotism, the didactics of Aristotle, Freud, Comparative Religion, and the belief in family unity.

4. **TITLE:**   EXPERIENCE MY BEFRIENDED IDEAL

YEAR: 1996

PRICE: £7-50

ISBN: 0 9527253 0 4

DESCRIPTION: This anthology consists of metaphysical poems, verses with philosophical simplicity and romantic compositions.

5. **TITLE:**   JOYFUL PARENTING

YEAR: 1997

PRICE: £12-50

ISBN: 0 9527956 1 2

DESCRIPTION: The psychology of child culture. Pre-natal, post-natal and all stages of development.

6. **TITLE:**   THE MANAGEMENT OF COMMERCIAL COMPUTING

YEAR: 1996

PRICE: £25

ISBN: 0 9527956 0 4

DESCRIPTION: The development and management of systems and people in multi-national corporations, systems and software houses, government departments, European Union Commissions and academia.

7. **TITLE:**   BUSINESS INFORMATION SYSTEMS, CONCEPTS AND EXAMPLES

YEAR: 1998

PRICE: £35

ISBN: 0 9527956 3 9

DESCRIPTION: This book aims to fill a gap in the current business and tutorial literature. It has been designed for the business individual, for the student and the computer professional who need a detailed overview of business information systems. It explores computing in general, the structured development of systems using processes and data analysis; object oriented and other methods. It includes the project planning and testing procedures for the Millennium thread.

8. TITLE:	A GUIDE TO INFORMATION TECHNOLOGY
YEAR:	1999
PRICE:	£12-50
ISBN:	0 9527956 4 7
DESCRIPTION:	The book covers the fundamental aspects of computing and the development of new information systems. Explains the current systems, structured analysis and designing, management, planning and other problems and solutions.

9. TITLE:	TRADING ON THE INTERNET IN THE YEAR 2000 AND BEYOND
YEAR:	1999
PRICE:	£12-50
ISBN:	0 9527956 7 1
DESCRIPTION:	Use of the Internet and E-Commerce is a business issue first and foremost. The Information Superhighway will see the consumer having access to a myriad of data through the PC or TV screen. The digital market is so extensive that most retailers will establish the marketplace by designing around a number of architectural models. The design of the system will be based on how the users work and what suits the overall business environment.

10. TITLE:	THE SIGMA METHODOLOGY FOR RISK MANAGEMENT IN SYSTEMS DEVELOPMENT
YEAR:	
PRICE:	February, 2002
	£19-50
ISBN:	0 9527956 8 X
DESCRIPTION:	The Sigma methodology allows the capture of collective knowledge and expertise from those involved on the project, in a form that facilitates communication of Events, Assessments and the pro-active management of Risks. Sigma can be applied to any type of project, or programme.

11. TITLE:	THE MANAGEMENT OF PROJECTS, SYSTEMS, INTERNET AND RISKS
YEAR:	
PRICE:	March, 2002
	£50
ISBN:	0 9527956 9 8
DESCRIPTION:	The Programme/Project Management methods described in this book provide a generic structure for the development of IT systems, Project Management techniques and how to plan projects. Useful to Programme and Project Managers, Analysts, Designers, Programmers, Executives, Academics and Students.

12. TITLE:	THE PROJECT MANAGEMENT PROCEDURES FOR SYSTEMS DEVELOPMENT
YEAR:	March 2002
PRICE:	£12-50
ISBN:	0 9527 253 1 2
DESCRIPTION:	Projects are conceived and grow from a business need, but what seems clear at the beginning often becomes blurred and confused. In the end projects may not deliver what was expected and costly investment produces few benefits. The PROJECT MANAGEMENT PROCEDURES FOR SYSTEMS DEVELOPMENT method described in this book provides a generic model product breakdown structure for an IT system down to the third level, which gives a starting point for project-specific planning.

13. TITLE:	I.T. RISK MANAGEMENT
YEAR:	August 2002
PRICE:	£12-50
ISBN:	0 9527 253 2 0

DESCRIPTION: A risk is an uncertain event, which may have an adverse effect on the project's objectives. This book explains a proven risk management methodology, which should be very effective in the quest for identifying risks throughout the project lifecycle. It describes the processes, which commence by identifying the enterprise's most important and risky projects, as these must be given priority. The book is, essentially, dealing with a method that permits the collection of knowledge and experience from those involved.

14. TITLE: MORAL PHILOSOPHY, THE ETHICAL APPROACH THROUGH THE AGES

YEAR: March 2003

PRICE: £33

ISBN: 0 9527 253 3 9

DESCRIPTION: This book on Moral Philosophy and Ethics deals with moral judgments and moral principles. It explains the applications as an extension of the meaning of ethics. It refers not to morality itself but to the field of study, or branch of inquiry, that has morality as its subject matter. In this writings ethics are viewed as a branch of philosophy and its all-embracing practical nature links it with many other areas of study, including anthropology, biology, medicine, economics, history, politics, psychology, sociology, and theology.

15. TITLE: FRONT-END DESIGN AND DEVELOPMENT FOR SYSTEMS APPLICATIONS

YEAR: September 2003

PRICE: £12-50

ISBN: 0 9527 253 4 7

DESCRIPTION: A guide to designing and developing the 'front-end' for systems applications, including the standards and guidelines for the Graphical User Interface (GUI) and the Human Computer Interface (HCI), through which users communicate with the computer system and the database. Also, dialogue styles in which a user is provided with a hierarchically organized set of choices pointing to and interacting with visible elements.

16. TITLE   CHANGE MANAGEMENT IN I.T.

YEAR: May 2004

PRICE: £12-50

ISBN: 0 9527 253 5 5

DESCRIPTION: Change Management and the changes to Configuration, Release and Assets as a whole group of activities have traditionally been concerned with finding effective solutions to specific operational problems. The purpose of this book is to look at current problems and new, better methods, techniques, and tools for processing changes.

17. TITLE   THE PHILOSOPHICAL CONCEPTS OF MANAGEMENT THROUGH THE AGES

YEAR: MARCH 2005

PRICE: £25

ISBN: 0 9527 253 6 3

DESCRIPTION: The process of managing a team involves the interaction of people where individuals contribute to the running or completion of a task. As in any State or country, under any government, people live together under various laws, rules, regulations and religions. The people elect or they follow a leader, be it a democratic or tyrannical leadership. People under such regimes follow a type of management. In a business environment such methods of management prevail. A Manager will delegate and lead one or more individuals within the organization by running the business or a system. Management styles can, therefore, be considered as political systems where people participate in the smooth running of a country or a company, whether this is a global organization or a fruit stall in the back streets of any city.

FRONT-END DESIGN AND DEVELOPMENT FOR SYSTEMS APPLICATIONS

A guide to designing and developing the 'front-end' for systems applications, including the standards and guidelines for the Graphical User Interface (GUI) and the Human Computer Interface (HCI), through which users communicate with the computer system and the database. Also, dialogue styles in which a user is provided with a hierarchically organised set of choices pointing to and interacting with visible elements.

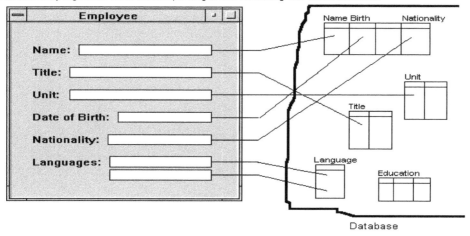

FIGURE 2.4 - DATABASE ORGANISATION IS TRANSPARENT TO THE USER

EurIng Prof Dr **Andreas Sofroniou**

Born in Morphou, Cyprus, Andreas holds the degrees of *Doctor of Psychology, Executive MBA* and *Doctor of Philosophy.* Also, qualifications as a *chartered member and fellow* of eighteen British professional institutions, including Engineering, Systems, Computing, Directing, Complementary Medicine, Management, Production, Programming, Marketing, Petroleum, Data Processing, Psychotherapy and Counselling. A *Research Life Fellow and Professor* of American Institutes and a member of working parties in the United Kingdom and Europe on systems and therapy.

Other studies included *Children's Art and Psychotherapy, Mental Illness/Mental Health and Advanced Psychological Topics.* A British Association for Counselling *Accredited Counsellor* holds various professional *fellowships* in England, Europe and the United States of America. Andreas established his first *therapeutic clinic* in 1973. Since then, he continued practising as a *Psychoanalyst, Psychotherapist, Counsellor and Philosophical Therapist* in various cities of the United Kingdom. The current *President* of the Association for Psychological Counselling and Training, a position held since 1982.

During his varied career, Andreas held the positions of *Overseas Marketing Executive, Production and Inventory Manager, Group Senior Systems Consultant, European Systems Manager and Principal Technical Adviser* with the multi-national organisations of International Computers Limited (ICL), Pitney Bowes, Plessey (GEC), Raychem and the Engineering Industry Training Board (EITB). For twenty years the *Managing Director* of PsySys Limited, a consultancy responsible for the development of systems, management and people. PsySys' list of clients includes international companies, software houses, European Union Commissions and British Government Departments. More recently, a *Programmes Director* for the European, Middle East and African (EMEA) and the Global Project Management divisions of Electronic Data Systems (EDS).

Participated as an *information technology expert* to the European Union and as a *therapeutic psychologist* to the Institute of Psychology and Parapsychology and the Harley Street Centre, London. A *published writer, poet and trainer*, the subjects include *Computing, Systems Methodology, Management, Psychotherapy and Therapeutic Philosophy.* Many articles were published on the Internet for the international readership. The subjects covered *Business Systems Management, Information Technology, Philosophic Counselling, Child Psychology and Poetry.* A number of extracts from his published books, articles and poems appeared under http://www.themestream.com. For achievements in *Systems Engineering, Psychology and Directing*, his biographical records are included in the directory of *'Who's Who In The World'*, published by Marquis of America and other international biographical publications. In 2001, nominated for *House of Lords membership* (non-political). In January 2003, together with PsySys Limited, was presented with the Achievement Award for twenty years of continued growth and client satisfaction. In July 2003, elected as one of the ten members of the Board of Advisors of the Trinity Southern University, Texas, USA.

FRONT-END DESIGN AND DEVELOPMENT FOR SYSTEMS APPLICATIONS
ISBN: 0 9527 253 4 7
Author: EurIng Prof Dr Andreas Sofroniou

www.ingramcontent.com/pod-product-compliance
Lightning Source LLC
Chambersburg PA
CBHW060457060326
40689CB00020B/4557